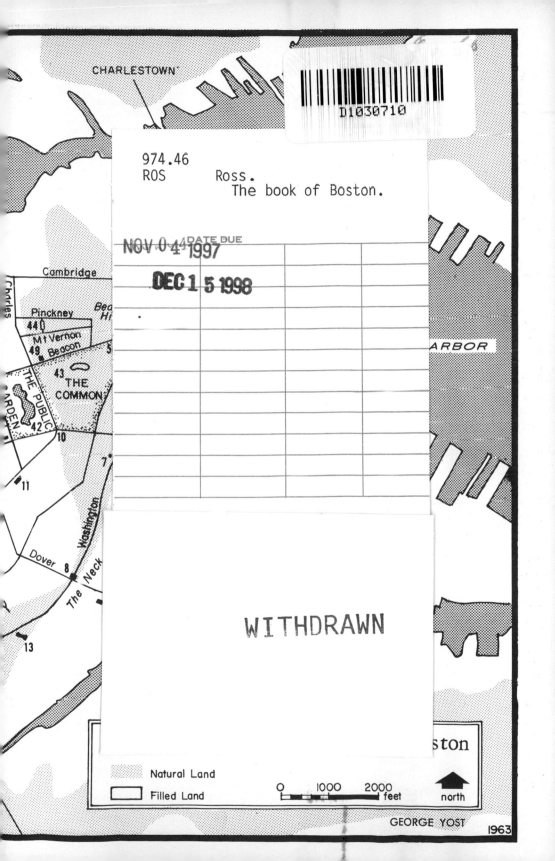

974.46
ROS   Ross.
            The book of Boston.

CHARLESTOWN

Cambridge

Pinckney
44
Mt Vernon
49 Beacon
43
THE
COMMON
42
10
7
11

Washington

Dover 8

The Neck

13

ARBOR

...ston

Natural Land

Filled Land

0   1000   2000
              feet   north

GEORGE YOST

1963

D1030710

THE BOOK OF BOSTON

The Boston Public Library

The Book of
BOSTON

THE VICTORIAN PERIOD
1837 to 1901

By MARJORIE DRAKE ROSS

With photographs by Samuel Chamberlain

HASTINGS HOUSE PUBLISHERS

New York

To

MY HUSBAND

John Clifford Ross

AND MY SON

John Drake Ross

This Book is
Affectionately Inscribed

CONTENTS

ACKNOWLEDGMENTS

The following sources have been drawn upon in the compiling of this book. The author is very grateful for them.

Algonquin Club of Boston, Its Early History, 1886–1961. Boston: 1961

Beebe, Lucius Morris, *Mr. Pullman's Elegant Palace Car.* Garden City: Doubleday and Company, 1961

Boston Symphony Orchestra Program, Page 1508 Boston: 1959–1960 Season

Carter, Morris, *Isabella Stewart Gardner and Fenway Court.* Boston: Houghton Mifflin Company, 1940

Carver, Robin, *Stories About Boston.* Boston: Lilly, Wait and Company, 1832

Crawford, Mary Caroline, *Romantic Days in Old Boston.* Boston: Little, Brown and Company, 1910

Dickens, Charles, *American Notes.* New York: 1847. London 1874

Drake, Samuel Adams, *Old Landmarks of Boston.* Boston: James R. Osgood and Company, 1875. Late Ticknor & Fields, and Fields, Osgood & Co.

Earle, Alice Morse, *Stage Coach and Tavern Days.* London: Macmillan Company, 1900

Emerson, Edward Waldo, *The Early Years of the Saturday Club.* Boston: Houghton Mifflin Company, 1918

Encyclopaedia Britannica, 11th Edition, Cambridge, England: 1910–1911

Engelhardt, George W., *Boston Massachusetts.* Boston: Chamber of Commerce, 1897

Farmer, Fanny Merritt, *The Boston Cooking-School Cook Book.* Boston: Little, Brown and Company, 1896.

First Corps of Cadets, Records. Boston: 1944

Forbes, Allan and Eastman, Ralph M., *Some Statues of Boston.* Boston: State Street Trust Company, 1946

Groce, George C. and Walace, David H., *Dictionary of Artists in America.* New Haven: Yale University Press, 1957

Holmes, Oliver Wendell, *The Autocrat of the Breakfast Table.* Boston: James R. Osgood and Company, 1872

Howe, Henry F., *Massachusetts, There She Is Behold Her.* New York: Harpers Brothers, 1960

Howe, M. A. deWolfe, *Boston Common, Scenes from Four Centuries*. Cambridge: The Riverside Press, 1910

Howe, M. A. deWolfe, *Boston, The Place and The People*. New York: Macmillan Company, 1903

Howe, M. A. deWolfe, *Memories of a Hostess*. Boston: The Atlantic Monthly Press, 1922

Kilham, Walter H., *Boston After Bulfinch*. Cambridge: Harvard University Press, 1946

King, Moses, *King's Hand Book of Boston*. Cambridge: Moses King Publisher, 1883

Lee, Sir Sidney, *Dictionary of National Biography*. London: The Macmillan Company, 1912

Mackenzie, Catherine, *Alexander Graham Bell*. New York: Grosset and Dunlap, 1928

Mann, Albert W., *Walks and Talks about Historic Boston*. Boston: Mann Publishing Company, 1917

Mann, Dorothea Lawrance, *The Story of The Old Corner Book Store*. Boston: *The Transcript*, 1928

McCord, David, *About Boston, Sight, Sound, Flavor & Inflection*. Boston: Little, Brown & Company, 1948

Payne, Edward F., *Dickens' Day in Boston*. Cambridge: Houghton Mifflin, The Riverside Press, 1927

Proceedings of The Bostonian Society. Boston: Old State House, 1952

Spears, John R., *The Story of the New England Whalers*.

Stark, James H., *Stark's Antique Views of ye Towne of Boston*. Boston: 1901

Whitehill, Walter Muir, *Boston A Topographical History*. Cambridge: The Belnap Press of Harvard University Press, 1959

Whipple, A. B. C., *Tall Ships and Great Captains*. New York: Harper Brothers, 1951

Winsor, Justin, *The Memorial History of Boston*. Boston: Charles Little and James Brown, 1846

Withey, Henry F. and Elsie, *Dictionary of American Architects*. Los Angeles: New Age Publishing Company, 1956

LIST OF ILLUSTRATIONS

List of Illustrations

List of Illustrations

List of Illustrations

List of Illustrations

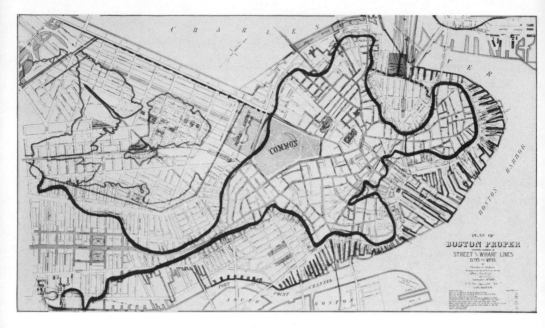

Plan of Boston proper showing changes in street and wharf lines,
1795–1895

The Book of
BOSTON

THE VICTORIAN PERIOD
1837-1901

BOSTON has one of the most fascinating histories of any American city. From this hub the great spokes of industry and culture have reached out to all parts of our land. Boston is not just another city but the nucleus of our rich heritage.

THE COLONIAL PERIOD

Founded in 1630 by Governor Winthrop's small band of pioneers, many of whom had migrated from Boston, England, the settlement soon grew into a thriving colonial town. †
It nestled on the water front, resembling a sleepy English village, and overlooked a beautiful harbor dotted with small islands. Picturesque lanes and crooked byways, several of which remain, led to the market place, the First Church, and "a sweet spring." This site is still called Spring Lane. * The First Town House was nearby on King Street, now State Street. * Here in this wooden building the General Court held its monthly meetings above the market stalls. The un-

† See the *Book of Boston — The Colonial Period.*
‡ See the *Book of Boston — The Federal Period.*
* Historic site or building now standing.
** Historic site or building open to visitors.

painted frame dwelling houses with their overhanging upper stories, Tudor gables, and diamond-paned casement windows reflected medieval England. Constructed of local materials, these houses exemplified our early American style of architecture.

From these humble beginnings in the Colonial South End the town spread to the North End. Docks, shops, and more homes were built. Each settler had his plot of land, a small town farm, surrounding his dwelling. One of these farmhouses still stands, known as the Paul Revere House, ** where the patriot silversmith made his home from 1770 to 1800.

During the eighteenth century Boston grew and prospered. Larger homes, churches, more public buildings, and wharves were built. Some, like the Old State House, ** which replaced the First Town House, were of brick in the English early Georgian style. Many of these fine colonial structures exist today, dear to the hearts of all Americans as symbols and sites of our struggle for freedom. †

THE EARLY FEDERAL PERIOD

After the Revolutionary War Boston entered her second great phase. This was a period of adjusting from an English colonial village to an important town influential in the development of the new republic.

Boston merchant ships sailed to many ports in China, India, Europe, and the West Indies. The trade made huge fortunes. With this prosperity came an era of gracious living.

Many of our early American heroes and patriots had come from colonial Boston. Now she gave to the nation other great men, among them statesmen, merchants, and our first eminent architect, Charles Bulfinch.

Influenced by the taste and excellent town planning of Bulfinch, Boston became a town of red-brick houses of the late Georgian style with tree-shaded streets and squares. Merchants built large mansions on Beacon Hill * and along Summer Street which they enriched with fine Hepplewhite and Sheraton-style furniture and adorned with porcelains from China. ‡

In this early federal period Bulfinch designed the beautiful Massachusetts State House ** which still crowns Beacon Hill. This noble building with its dome and portico set a fashion for other capitol buildings in the new states. Bulfinch was also the architect of many fine churches and homes.

About the time that Boston became a city in 1822 the Greek Revival style came into vogue. Several of these distinguished buildings were built of granite from recently opened quarries in the vicinity. The last building designed by Bulfinch in Boston was in this style and of this material. This classic edifice, known now as the *Bulfinch Building*, ** was the original building of the Massachusetts General Hospital, the beginning of our great medical center.

THE VICTORIAN PERIOD

Shortly after the two hundredth anniversary of the first settlement Boston entered her third great period of development. Gone was the quiet, simple, slow-moving life of colonial farming and churchgoing, the era of busy artisans, and the leisurely, gracious living of the early federal merchants. The Industrial Revolution changed the old Boston way of life. With the coming of a new sense of values, wealth became a symbol of success.

In these years of the nineteenth century the city again reflected European influences, especially those from Victorian

View of Boston from Dorchester Heights, now South Boston
Engraving by Robert Havell

England and the Second Empire in France. New developments forecast the future. All over the world life was gathering momentum. Victorian Boston began to throb to the pulse of the age and each decade brought something new.

The advent of the machine replaced hand labor, brought in new techniques, and speeded up production. This resulted in many changes and created new classes of society: the industrialists and the factory workers.

Many new types of business were established, and with their expansion and prosperity, banking developed.

Science progressed and inventions succeeded one another rapidly, making life easier though more complex.

Family life was disciplined with high standards and a rigid moral code. Duty came before pleasure. It was a serious age with emphasis on personal industry, integrity, and education.

During these years Boston became the metropolis of New England, a city known and honored in the four corners of the earth as the "Athens of America."

Boston, the capital of the state of Massachusetts, well situated on Massachusetts Bay, was the hub of the increased activity. With its growth in size and stature came many radical changes. The neighboring towns of Roxbury, Dorchester, and Charlestown were incorporated into the city limits. Life became urban rather than rural as it had been in the two earlier centuries. The face of Boston changed from a busy, picturesque town to a thriving utilitarian city. A great business section downtown replaced the artisans' shops of earlier days and absorbed most of the old village and much of the fine federal residential district south of the Common. With the Victorian era came the development of the railroad, the large factories, big business, and the resulting wealth and pov-

Residence of Thomas G. Appleton Esq., 10 Commonwealth Avenue
Nathan Appleton Esq., in the "Victoria" carriage

erty. These changes introduced new types of transportation, industry, and architecture. Iron replaced wood in the hulls of ships and in the structure of bridges and buildings.

Transportation

Methods of transportation changed rapidly, but the horse was still used to draw a variety of vehicles. The clop, clop of horses' hoofs was a familiar sound. Some of the streets were straightened and others were widened and paved with bricks or granite blocks. A few of the latter still remain in Haymarket Square * and near the Quincy Market. **

New types of private and public carriages, as well as commercial wagons, tipcarts, and drays clattered along the newly improved roads. Family carriages were often elegantly equipped and drawn by pairs of beautifully groomed horses in fine leather harnesses ornamented with polished metal. Some carriages were imported from England and others were made here in the European style. Ladies rode about in their open "victorias" holding tiny carriage parasols tilted to shade them from the sun. They were driven by silk-hatted liveried coachmen sitting erect. The coachmen's coats often matched the carriage robes and the Turkish tufted and buttoned upholstery of plum, black, or fawn-colored broadcloth. A long black whip was a necessary piece of equipment, either held in the driver's hand or in a black leather socket on the dashboard. These shiny, black, four-wheeled pleasure vehicles had collapsible tops, flat mudguards, and carriage lamps at each side.

In winter the coachman sometimes carried a pottery bottle in the shape of his own figure dressed in a tall hat and caped greatcoat from which a "nip" now and then warmed him as he waited in the cold for his master or mistress. The ladies carried a small pottery hot-water bottle of prayer-book shape in their tiny muffs to keep their hands warm.

Gentlemen belonged to driving clubs where harness racing in sulkies with trotting horses was popular. One of these driving clubs with its track could be seen until recently beside the Charles River in Cambridge. This is now the site of the Museum of Contemporary Art ** and the Cambridge Drama Center.

Both ladies and gentlemen drove themselves in stylish gigs or two-wheeled one-horse carriages. Closed carriages, called broughams, were popular for evening transportation. Public hacks, known as cabs, were for hire at railroad stations and hotels. Hansom cabs, named for the Englishman who invented them, had one horse, two wheels, and a protective hood. The driver sat high on a box in the rear. These were popular at the end of the period and are still used in Central Park in New York City.

Blacksmith shops were busy places, and public livery stables were large and prosperous businesses. Mansions and town houses had private stables with elaborate stalls and sheathed and varnished harness rooms. Each horse's name, usually lettered in gold, was placed above its stall. Collections of ribbons and trophies won by these treasured animals were often displayed in glass-enclosed cases on the walls. Large picturesque stables and barns on the suburban estates and in the country had a tall weather vane mounted on the ridge or above a decorative cupola. In town, on lower Chestnut Street, at the foot of Beacon Hill, there were many small private brick stables which have since been converted into homes. Consequently, that part of this fashionable street was known in the Victorian period as "Horse-Chestnut Street."

In the winter sleighs and delivery pungs glided over the hard-packed snow on smooth iron runners. Children could not resist a pung ride, clinging to the rear and standing on the

A coachman's bottle, Bennington 1849

The Metropolitan Horse Railroad, Tremont Street, Boston, showing the Granary Burying Ground with the Tremont House at the right

The last horse car on Marlborough Street, 1900

runners. These boxlike sleighs were piled with hay and equipped with warm blankets when they were hired by groups of merry boys and girls for moonlight sleighrides.

Sleighing out Beacon Street and over the Mill Dam to the Brighton Road was a favorite sport. Driving their own sleighs, gentlemen in mink-lined black broadcloth coats and fur caps reined in their frisky mares. With sleighbells jingling and their ladies snugly tucked in beside them in fur robes, they enjoyed a ride in the cold, invigorating air of the old-fashioned New England winters.

Commercial teams and wagons were drawn by large, strong work horses, picturesque with long hair fringing their hoofs. In summer they wore straw hats pierced for their ears and net blankets of string to keep off the flies. In winter woolen horse blankets kept them warm as they waited for their loads or enjoyed a bucket of oats.

29

Open trolley cars on Tremont Street with the Park Street Church in the background

Large and decorative watering troughs of cast iron, each with a pedestal supporting a basin at a convenient height for horses to drink, dotted the city. Many had low watering places for dogs as well.

Streetcars traversed the city except on Beacon Hill and were first drawn by horses. These horsecars, in use in the last half of the nineteenth century, were painted different colors to indicate their route and were also equipped with designation signs. In the winter they had hay on the floor to keep the passengers' feet warm.

Trolley cars succeeded the horse railroads. They ran along iron car tracks in the middle of the street and were propelled by electricity. This caused them to be called "the electrics." The current was conducted through a trolley from an overhead wire that sometimes slid off and stalled the car. This gave rise to the humorous comment of the day, "He's off his trolley."

Open cars were put into service during the summer months. These were equipped with long, horizontal wooden seats protected from the rain by striped drop awnings. Excursions out of town to the Blue Hills, City Point, and elsewhere were popular.

The motormen who drove the cars were friendly with the passengers, often waiting for the regular riders, especially the young beaux who came running to catch the last car home at night.

When downtown Boston became congested, elevated tracks for electric trains were built high up on iron trestles over the surface traffic. They traveled from Forest Hills to Sullivan Square above Washington Street and the newly made Atlantic Avenue. Known as "the El," these speedy and convenient trains of cars ran on two tracks with the electricity

Dover Street Elevated Station, Boston

in a third rail. The Dover Street Station, one of the few remaining in its original state, with high covered iron steps and a waiting platform, may be seen from the exit of the southeast expressway at Dover Street.

Later in the century the subway was constructed. Trolley cars left the surface to go underground opposite the Public Garden at Arlington Street, on Cambridge Street and other points. When the subway was begun, Moses King in *How to See Boston*, published in 1898, said "It will be watertight, brilliantly lighted, and perfectly ventilated, and warmer in winter and cooler in summer than the surface streets." This great engineering feat helped to bring people rapidly to the center of the city and was a marked improvement over the slow surface traffic.

Although steam trains came to Boston in the 1830's, it was much later in the nineteenth century before the railroads became the great transportation system of the age. They connected Boston with the West and brought the latter in more direct touch with Europe by way of the Atlantic seaports. Although the few existing turnpikes and canal boats were still in use, the bulk of the huge new commerce in foods and other commodities was hauled by long freight trains. Bostonians invested heavily in these railroads and more wealth came to the city in return.

The early trains were composed of a series of cars in the shape of stagecoaches, each carrying eight passengers, and drawn by wood-fired steam engines. Coal later replaced wood fuel. This means of travel was crowded and uncomfortable. The seats were hard, the cars had no springs, and some of the passengers had to ride backward. The "iron horse" belched forth sparks and sometimes set fire to the countryside. The shrill tooting of the whistle scattered animals and people. The

Boston from the southwest; drawn by J. W. Barber, showing steam trains crossing the waters of the Back Bay on causeways, with Beacon Hill, the State House, and Boston Common

unaccustomed speed of about eighteen miles an hour seemed excessive. To ride on these trains was a dangerous and frightening experience.

The first steam trains, known as "the cars," came into Boston across the waters of the Back Bay over a rickety open wooden structure rightly called "Dizzy Bridge."

By 1844 the causeways carried the roadbeds across this water, greatly decreasing the feeling of suspense as one approached the city.

From these beginnings much of the great railroad system of America developed. As time went on iron became a very important material for structure and equipment. Large, picturesque bridges of arch and lattice patterns supported the tracks over the highways and waterways. Later steam trains had more efficient locomotives and more comfortable cars. Besides the regular passenger cars there were those for ladies, for mail, and for smoking. Iron stoves warmed them in winter.

In 1867 there were luxurious "parlor cars" with elaborately upholstered chairs and colorful carpets. Sleeping cars called "Pullmans," for George Mortimer Pullman who invented them, were fitted with seats which were converted into beds at night. Tycoons traveled in their own private cars attached to the rear of regular trains. These cars had sentimental Victorian names such as "Violet," "Pansy," "Aurora," and "Niagara Falls." Others were named for the presidents, or towns and cities. Luxurious and fast "crack" trains also had names. "The Dude," a private train with a fancy engine ornamented with brass, carried summer residents back and forth from Cape Cod to Boston daily in the summer season. Other special trains ran to the North Shore and to other New England resorts.

34

Interior view of a New York, New Haven and Hartford Railroad parlor car, running out of Boston

Iron railroad bridge

The interiors of the cars became increasingly ornate. Many were complete with heavy silk draperies, beveled-edge plate-glass mirrors, rich carpets, red plush upholstery, antimacassars, hassocks, palms, cuspidors, and gas lights. One may be seen at the Edaville Railroad Museum in Carver, Massachusetts. The "sleepers" were equipped with upper and lower berths curtained in heavy green material and were served by Negro porters. A drawing room was available in each Pullman car for those who wished greater privacy. There was also a small room at the end of each car in which a washbasin and a water closet, known as the "W.C.," was provided. Dining cars were attached to the trains traveling longer distances. These were the last word in service and luxurious fittings. The tables were set with fine linen and fresh flowers. White-coated Negro waiters and chefs offered a menu of choice foods and wines and served the meals of four courses on many dishes.

Iron-supported glass-covered boarding platform (now much altered)

Jenny Lind

Huge passenger stations with long train sheds covered with iron-supported glass were erected to serve the several lines running into the city.

The old Fitchburg Railroad Station, designed by George M. Dexter and built on Causeway Street in 1847, was one of the most important. Set on land made when the colonial Mill Pond was filled in, it stood on the site of the present North Station. This granite building had towers and crenellations like a medieval fortress and a façade ornamented with a clock and a brass motif of an early locomotive now in the Edaville Railroad Museum. Inside the depot, on the floor above the concourse, was a large hall. Here Jenny Lind gave two of her famous concerts under the direction of P. T. Barnum. Four thousand people attended each of these recitals and were charmed by the beautiful voice of the Swedish singer. She was paid a thousand dollars for each concert, an enormous amount for those days!

The old Providence Station (demolished) Park Square, showing the
horse traffic and the Emancipation statue

The interesting Boston and Albany depot on Kneeland
Street was built of brick and stone, with an inner court covered by a glass skylight. The ladies' waiting room was handsomely "fitted up" and warmed by three fifteen-foot open
fireplaces.

38

The old Providence Station on Columbus Avenue at Park Square, where the Statler Hotel now stands, was noteworthy among the railroad depots in Boston. It was considered the most "completely appointed" (according to *King's Handbook of Boston* 1878–83), and "out of it ran the fastest train in the United States." This massive building had Gothic archways and a lofty tower with an illuminated clock. Beside the tracks were covered platforms. "Inside there were reading, dining, billiard, and smoking rooms as well as a barbershop and washrooms."

Public clocks like the one on the Providence Station became numerous. They not only appeared on railroad stations, factories, and public buildings, but were set up in front of business establishments. Many of these large clocks were made by the Howard Clock Company of Roxbury, and one of their sidewalk clocks mounted on its original tall iron post still serves the public on Boylston Street in front of Otis Clapp and Sons, Druggists.

Sidewalk clock, Boylston Street

Shipbuilding at East Boston, 1885, showing Bunker Hill Monument at the right

Shipping

The port of Boston continued to be busy and important in spite of the fact that New York was getting more and more of the marine trade by the 1840's. The East India and China trade continued to beckon. The discovery of gold in California greatly stimulated shipping. From 1844 to 1854 Boston led the country in foreign trade and its ships sailed to all parts of the world.

Its great merchant fleet was still operating under sail. The demand for speed brought a new type of fast sailing vessel, the great "clipper ships." The outstanding builder of these beautiful and swift clippers was Donald McKay. Of Scottish descent, he was born in 1810 at Shelburne, Nova

Ship figurehead, carved by Isaac Fowle

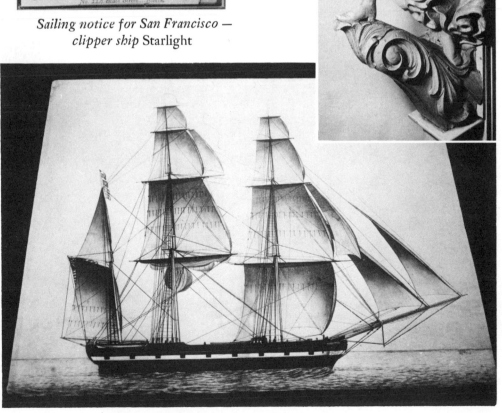

Sailing notice for San Francisco —
clipper ship Starlight

Canton packet ship

The clipper ship Lightning *of Liverpool, England, built at East Boston, 1854, by Donald McKay*

R.M.S. Persia *of the Cunard Line, combination steam and sailing ship*

Scotia, one of a family of eighteen children. At the age of sixteen he migrated to New York, then moved to Wiscasset, Maine, and finally to Newburyport, Massachusetts, where he found work and became a qualified shipwright. In 1844, at the age of thirty-four, he settled in East Boston and opened his own yard where he built packet ships.

In 1852 he launched the first of his famous clipper ships. These noble vessels were not only fast sailing, but also had a large cargo capacity. McKay's designs were impressive and his workmanship was always of the best. His clippers had a graceful, slender bow, ornamented with a carved, painted, and gilded figurehead, and a handsome display of snowy canvas. Under full sail they were majestically beautiful and were the fastest ships afloat. *The Flying Cloud* was the most renowned of all. On her maiden voyage in 1851 she rounded Cape Horn and sailed to the port of San Francisco from New York in eighty-nine days, in spite of many storms and other hazards. His *Lightning* was the fastest sailing ship ever built.

In 1852 he built the *Sovereign of the Seas*. Like all the other clippers, she made a fortune for her owner, netting McKay $135,000 on her first voyage. In 1853 the *Great Republic*, McKay's masterpiece, the largest of the clipper ships, slid down the ways.

Some of these great three-masted, square-rigged clippers sailed to Calcutta, Canton, and many other ports in the East bringing home a variety of cargoes. Although the great age of clipper ships was the 1850's, they remained in service until the 1870's and continued to pay huge profits.

In 1875 Donald McKay closed his yard and retired. A granite shaft was erected at Castle Island, Boston, to memorialize his work and inscribed: "Master-Builder, whose genius produced ships of a beauty and speed before unknown which swept the Seven Seas, made the American Clipper Ship famous the world over, and brought renown and prosperity to the City of Boston."

After 1838 steamships came into use along with many new types of vessels. The change from sail to steam power and from hulls of wood to those of iron was very slow. In 1840 the Cunard Steamship Line established regular service between Boston and England. Some of these earliest steamers were equipped with sails as well as engines. These furnished greater speed, stability, and security, as the motors were often faulty.

The Cunard liner, *Persia*, was one of these combination sail-and-steamships equipped with single-screw paddles or side wheels. She achieved a speed of 12.5 knots. In 1856 she set out on her maiden voyage, the first "iron steamer" in the

R.M.S. Britannia *ice bound in Boston Harbor, 1844,*
John Hewitt, commander

Boston Harbor and shipping from the State Street block

Atlantic service of the Cunard Line. As this type of shipping increased, Boston Harbor resounded with steamboat whistles along with the sound of flapping sails.

New England winters are always formidable, but the winter of 1844 was more severe than usual. The harbor froze solid from the wharves to the lighthouse. Eventually ice cutters, hardy men from Fresh Pond in Cambridge, used iron saws to open a channel seven miles long to free the imprisoned ships. In later years steamboats, known as icebreakers, replaced these men.

Gradually the face of Boston Harbor changed again. The smokestacks of ocean-going steam vessels, with their clouds of black smoke silhouetted against the horizon, mingled with the forest of masts of sailing ships and the clock towers of churches and other buildings beyond.

As shipping interests, both passenger and freight, expanded, wharves were improved and new ones built. By the 1880's there were two hundred of these spacious quays, and the water front was alive with activity.

Among those remaining is *T Wharf*, a "T"-shaped addition to the old colonial Long Wharf. The name refers to the shape and has nothing to do with tea or the historic "Boston Tea Party." At one time it handled part of the great trade which made the Boston fish industry the largest in the world.

Commercial Wharf, of granite with a massive block of fifty-four stores four stories high, was one of the finest quays. Nearby, on the other docks, great ranges of warehouses * were also built. These solid granite buildings were the pride of the city, and were unexcelled in the world. They are still in use and may be seen near the Custom House as you drive along the overhead expressway.

Railroad spur tracks and freight yards, in addition to grain and coal elevators near the wharves, facilitated the increased shipping along the water front. The railroads and shipping companies brought great fortunes to Victorian Boston.

In the fifties more filling in of the shoreline, coves, and bays created land for warehouses, railroad stations, and the dwellings needed to accommodate the rapidly increasing commerce and population. Between 1868 and 1870 some of the old docks were covered with earth taken from Fort Hill to make land for Atlantic Avenue. This wide new street, about one hundred feet across, paved with granite-block cobblestones, absorbed the old shoreline. At that time the waters of

46

the harbor came up to the present India and Broad streets, but soon the site of "The Boston Tea Party" at Griffin's wharf nearby was covered with fill to make the land for the laying out of these new streets. India and Central wharves, both recently demolished, were built out beyond this extended water front. By the 1850's Commercial Wharf was the largest dock and the center of the grain trade. Commercial Street led to this wharf and, on the days when a ship cast off, the area was so crowded that the street was impassable.

Sailing notice Australian Line

In the 1880's the deep-water harbor swarmed with packets, ferries, barges, new steam tugs, and many other craft. There was also a steam fireboat equipped with four pumps. Pilot boats, considered the most efficient in the world, safely guided the numerous ships in and out of the long harbor, past the many small picturesque islands.

Inland waterways and the railroads brought products to Boston from the ever-increasing industrial centers. The Middlesex Canal, ‡ the first and most important, was used until 1851 to bring cotton goods from the mills of the Merrimack Valley for distribution and shipment abroad.

The splendid granite Custom House ** had been built on the water front in 1848. This fine Greek Revival building † by Ammi B. Young (1800–74), impressive with its great monolithic columns, became inadequate for the needs of the extraordinary shipping business.

A tall, square tower, five hundred feet high, with a clock, was added, replacing the original dome. This provided the needed space for offices with good light and air and did not detract from the building except for the loss of the dome. Although this building is inland today, a light at the top of the tower may be seen far out at sea, announcing Boston to incoming ships and planes.

*The Custom House with the tower added. The Grain and Flour
Building in French Gothic style at right*

Factory showing steam train and oxen-drawn cars

Industries

The 1840's brought the Industrial Revolution and further business expansion. As the factory system developed the social order changed. Personal contact between the artisan and the apprentice was replaced by the more impersonal relationship of capital and labor. Many of the new companies were financed by the sale of shares to stockholders, while some were still privately owned. The craftsman gave way to the factory worker. The ready-made replaced the handmade, especially in the clothing business, and the machine produced quantity rather than quality.

Many new products and processes were introduced at this time. Rubber imported from India was made into fire hose, waterproof clothing, and tires for bicycles and carriages. The boot and shoe business became one of the largest industries in Massachusetts. Foundries made iron pipes, stoves, furnaces, elevators, locomotives, marine engines and sewing machines in large quantities. Old companies as well as the newly founded businesses expanded and installed the latest machinery. Power looms increased the manufacture of cloth. Towns surrounding the city built great mills of brick and stone beside the rivers. Large painted wooden factories, often with a clock tower, stretched out along the railroad tracks. Numerous inventions brought new methods, tools, and machinery. Patents now protected the inventors. Steam first and then electricity replaced water power. The increased use of soft coal in industry and transportation blackened the once-green countryside.

Most of the new industries grew up beyond the city limits with the result that Boston, unlike many large cities, did not have concentrated factory areas except in South and East Boston. It became an industrial capital and mercantile outlet for the outlying mills and factories. The Boston offices of these companies were located in special sections of the city, such as the wool and leather centers. The State Street area became a great banking district.

More and more people worked here in offices, railroad terminals, warehouses, and the new department stores. With this influx and activity came poverty as well as added prosperity.

The migration from the farms of New England to the cities, and the flow of immigration from abroad, created congested working and living conditions.

The potato famines in Ireland during 1845 and 1846 forced many people to seek a livelihood elsewhere. Thousands

Portrait of the young Charles Dickens painted in Boston, 1842, by Francis Alexander (1800–81). (Right) William Makepeace Thackeray

of Irish immigrants came to Boston. Unskilled and poor, they accepted menial work and settled in overpopulated districts, at first principally in the North End and later in the South End. These and other people with foreign customs swept aside the old Boston traditions and transformed whole regions of the city.

In spite of this overcrowding Boston was one of the cleanest of the nineteenth-century cities. Charles Dickens (1812–70) in his *American Notes* describes this: "The houses were so bright and gay — the bricks were so very red, the stone was so very white, the blinds and area railings were so very green, the knobs and plates upon the street doors so marvelously bright and twinkling. . . . The city is a beautiful one, and cannot fail, I should imagine, to impress all strangers very favorably. The private dwelling-houses are, for the most part, large and elegant; the shops are extremely good; and the public buildings handsome."

The Golden Age
of Letters

In January, 1842, after a stormy, uncomfortable crossing of eighteen days on the steam packet *Britannia*, Mr. and Mrs. Charles Dickens arrived in Boston from England. They landed at Long Wharf at 5 P.M.

The next morning Dickens walked out from his hotel, the Tremont House, ‡ eager to see the city. Young, good-looking and enthusiastic, he became popular in Boston. No one had been so much sought after and feted since the visit of Lafayette in 1825.

Ten years later William Makepeace Thackeray (1811–63) came to Boston on the Cunard Line steamer *Canada*. He, too, stayed at the famous and luxurious Tremont House and was welcomed and widely entertained. Like Dickens, he returned for a second visit later, but these first visits were the most thrilling. Thackeray had crossed on the same ship with the poet James Russell Lowell, who later received him cordially at his home, Elmwood, * Cambridge. He also became the friend of William Hickling Prescott (1796–1859), the distinguished historian, and was often a guest in his home at 55 Beacon Street. * Both mansions still stand today.

In the mid-nineteenth century Boston was fortunate in having a notable group of authors many of whom were friends. Among these gentlemen was William Hickling Prescott, mentioned above. After graduating from Harvard and traveling abroad, he returned to this country to write. Encouraged by his friend, George Ticknor, a well-known Harvard professor and benefactor of the Boston Public Library, he became an eminent historian. In spite of increasing blindness he worked diligently for ten years on research for his *Ferdinand and Isabella*. This great work, published in 1837, made him famous.

In 1845 Prescott purchased 55 Beacon Street, ** a large, early federal house built in 1808 by the Boston architect, Asher Benjamin. Here in this stately home overlooking the Common and, at that time, the beautiful bay back of Boston, he set up his library on the second floor with his study above. This study, where he wrote, is said to have had some of the first large plate-glass windows in Boston. From the bay window he had an unobstructed view up Beacon Hill and of the beautiful trees in the neighboring back yards.

In this house for many years hung two Revolutionary swords (now in the Massachusetts Historical Society). One was carried by Prescott's grandfather, Colonel Prescott, in the battle of Bunker Hill; and the other by Mrs. Prescott's grandfather, Captain Linzee, who commanded the British sloop *Falcon* off Charlestown in the same battle. It is said that these swords (one drawn in the service of the Colonies and the other in the service of the King), seen by Thackeray during his many visits to this house, inspired him to write *The Virginians*, a story about two brothers who fought on opposite sides in the Revolutionary War.

The Prescotts' daughter, Elizabeth, was married in this house to the son of the Honorable and Mrs. Abbott Lawrence, then minister to the Court of St. James. A beautiful mauve-and-silver presentation gown, worn by Mrs. Lawrence when she was presented at Court in 1848, is still preserved in the house, in the costume collection of the National Society of the Colonial Dames of America in the Commonwealth of Massachusetts.

The Old Corner Book Store at the corner of School and Washington streets

In 1959, on the one hundredth anniversary of Prescott's death, a bronze portrait plaque by the eminent American sculptor, Joseph Coletti, was unveiled. This may be seen beside the entrance of the historian's home at 55 Beacon Street. *

George Ticknor (1791–1871) was a Bostonian who, after graduating from Dartmouth College, studied law and traveled abroad, then became professor of French and Spanish languages at Harvard. When he retired to devote himself to writing, he was succeeded in the professorship by Henry Wadsworth Longfellow (1807–82). Following the publication of his work, *The History of Spanish Literature*, in 1849, Ticknor employed himself largely in the interests of the Boston Public Library which he had been instrumental in founding. A pioneer in this field, he had the foresight to encourage the establishment of a free circulating library. He was also a generous donor of his time, means, and books. Like Prescott, his home was a beautiful old federal mansion on Beacon Hill. The house, still standing at the corner of Park and Beacon streets ‡ is now almost concealed by shop fronts. Here he housed his famous library of eighteen thousand volumes most of which were later presented to the Boston Public Library.

In 1832 William D. Ticknor, an able bookseller and printer, bought the old colonial brick dwelling house at the corner of School and Washington streets. In 1859 he and James Thomas Fields (1816–81) first published *The Atlantic Monthly*, a magazine which is still considered one of America's leading publications.

This building was also the headquarters of a brilliant group of Boston's literary figures who met in the "curtained corner" to discuss their own works and those of others.

Books were sold on the ground floor from 1825 to 1903, giving it the name *The Old Corner Book Store* † which it still bears. No other building, with the exception of the Boston Athenaeum, was more frequented by literary men and women browsing among the books.

This famous landmark, built in 1712, has recently been purchased by a newly formed, nonprofit organization, *Historic Sites, Inc.*, whose generous contributors made the preservation of this literary shrine possible.

In their home on Charles Street Mr. James Thomas Fields and his charming young wife gathered about them the eminent authors of the day. He encouraged writers and published their works. Several were among the early contributors to *The Atlantic Monthly*, and were celebrated for their other writings as well. Among them was Ralph Waldo Emerson (1803–82) whose essays began appearing in 1841; Nathaniel Hawthorne (1804–64) whose books included the

Statue of Ralph Waldo Emerson by Daniel Chester French

novel *The Scarlet Letter* which came out in 1850; and John
Greenleaf Whittier (1807–92), the Quaker poet, whose
Snow-Bound was published in 1866. Charles Dickens was a
frequent guest of James Fields, and during his second visit
to Boston they took brisk walks together about the city and
to Longfellow's house in Cambridge. The latter was a long
and often muddy journey by way of the West Boston Bridge
and Cambridgeport.

About town Dickens became a familiar figure in his
brown velvet-faced, long-coated suit and tall black silk hat.
A heavy gold watch chain stretched across the front of his
flowered vest was attached to a timepiece in his pocket. This
set a fashion and was known as a "Dickens watch chain." Some
men wore a gold "Albert" watch fob on a black grosgrain
ribbon hooked to a large pocket watch. These, and the long-
coated men's suits of these days, were named for Queen Victoria's consort, Prince Albert.

Many authors made their home in Boston or resided
there for a time. Beacon Hill was the favorite location and
most of their houses still stand. Henry Wadsworth Longfellow lived for a while at 3 West Cedar Street *; William
Dean Howells (1837–1920) at 4 Louisburg Square; * ‡ and
Thomas Bailey Aldrich (1836–1907) at 84 Pinckney Street *
when he wrote the *Story of a Bad Boy*. Dr. Oliver Wendell
Holmes (1809–94), a well-known wit, poet, and professor
of anatomy at the Harvard Medical School, after living on the
other side of the Common on Bosworth Street, came to 163
Charles Street, which he described as "the sunny street that
holds the sifted few."

Later he made his home in the newly developed Back
Bay section. Here on the waterside of Beacon Street at number 296, * in a brick-and-brownstone town house with the

The residence (1870) of Oliver Wendell Holmes, M.D.,
296 Beacon Street, Back Bay

usual angular bay window of the period, he spent his last
years. This house, much altered, still stands.

During the nineteenth century the status of women was
changing all over the world and Boston women were becoming prominent in public life. Some lived on Beacon Hill in
houses that remain there today. Among them was Julia Ward

Henry Wadsworth Longfellow

Howe (1819–1910), the wife of the lovable Dr. Samuel Gridley Howe (1801–76) who pioneered in helping the blind and the insane. She not only contributed to *The Atlantic Monthly*, but also wrote, among other poems, the words for *The Battle Hymn of the Republic*. The Howes lived for a while at number 13 Chestnut Street * on Beacon Hill in one of the fine early federal houses ‡ attributed to Bulfinch, and later at 241 Beacon Street in the Back Bay.

Louisa May Alcott (1832–88), who lived for a short time at 20 Pinckney Street * and then at 10 Louisburg Square, * ‡ wrote the popular novels *Little Men* and *Little Women* as well as articles in *The Atlantic Monthly*.

60

Julia Ward Howe, engraving by C. A. Powell

Harriet Beecher Stowe (1811–96) was another woman
who made her mark in this generation. Her remarkable book,
Uncle Tom's Cabin, was published in Boston in 1852. The
extraordinary response to this story of slave life stimulated the
cause of anti-slavery.

The Perkins Institute and Massachusetts Asylum for the Blind, South Boston, 1852, from Gleason's Pictorial, *July 24, 1852*

Statue of William Lloyd Garrison, by Olin L. Werner

The Anti-Slavery Movement

William Lloyd Garrison (1805–97), who had published his paper *The Liberator* since 1831, was now fervently seeking the abolition of slavery. Led by Garrison, Wendell Phillips, and Theodore Parker, Boston struck out again for liberty and worked diligently for the emancipation of the

William Ellery Channing   *Harriet Beecher Stowe*

Negroes. Anti-slavery societies were formed which sobered and inspired the public. Women came to the fore and worked passionately for the freeing of the four million Negroes. This movement focused attention on women in public life and led to their recognition in several other fields.

Many of the prominent thinkers in Boston at the time were Unitarians, most of whom wrote and spoke out against slavery. The tremendous growth of this denomination of liberal minds in the nineteenth century was a strong force in the community and the country. Numerous churches of different denominations had been absorbed by the Unitarians in Boston and all over New England. Some of their greatest leaders, among them Emerson and Channing, were preaching at this time.

Halls and Theaters

Architecture became urban, and new types of buildings were erected. Auditoriums were few until the Victorian era, but during this time many were built and used constantly for lectures, concerts, and fashionable dances.

The Music Hall was outstanding among them. Built in 1852 opposite the Park Street Church on Hamilton Place, it had an impressive interior and excellent acoustics. The great organ installed in 1863 was built by Walcker in Ludwigsburg near Stuttgart, Germany, at a cost of $60,000, and contained 5,474 pipes. It was the largest and finest in existence. The elaborate wooden case, designed by the architect, Hammatt Billings, (1818–75) was richly carved with caryatids and other figures in the round. It is still in use near Boston in the Methuen Music Hall.

The Victorian passion for sculpture was evident not only on the organ case but on the walls as well. Beneath the gas-lit cornice there were busts of composers on decorative brackets and a niche with a copy of the Apollo Belvedere. Three of these busts were the gifts of Charlotte Cushman, the Boston actress for whom the Charlotte Cushman Club was named.

The Music Hall was also the first Symphony Hall in Boston. The great orchestra, founded by Henry Lee Higginson in 1881 with sixty musicians, played here under the direction of George Henschel. Major Higginson, with his appreciation of music, realized the need for an established orchestra in the city and his generosity made it possible.

On February 24, 1882, Henschel conducted the Second Symphony of his intimate friend, Johannes Brahms. At the

Major Henry Lee Higginson, painted by John Singer Sargent

Interior of the Music Hall, showing the Great Organ

time this was highly controversial music not only here but abroad, and a good many in the audience departed after the second movement. The courageous and appreciative few remained. This is thought to be the origin of the term "Boston Brahmin" still applied to the cultured of the city.

The present Symphony Hall, designed by McKim, Mead, and White, was built in 1900 on Huntington Avenue when that district became the musical center of Boston. The auditorium is acoustically excellent and ranks among the three best in the world, the other two being Grosser Musikvereinsaal in Vienna and the Concertgebouw in Amsterdam. The interior, one of the most beautiful in Boston, is rich with carved and gilded Renaissance-classic ornament highlighting a quiet gray background. The niches with Greek and Roman statues and the pierced detail of the balcony fronts were carefully planned to aid the acoustics as well as add to the decorative scheme. It is a fitting setting for one of the world's most distinguished orchestras.

Here in the spring, after the symphony concert season is over, the famous Boston Pops series is given. These concerts of popular and classical music by members of the Boston Symphony Orchestra have been presented since 1885, first in the old Music Hall and then, as now, in Symphony Hall. The musicians play to an audience seated on gilt chairs around small tables where refreshments are served. The "Pops," as they are affectionately called, not only attract enthusiastic audiences every year but provide a longer season of employment for members of the orchestra.

Boston in the Victorian period became music minded. A beautiful opera house, the last of the great auditoriums of

Tremont Street from Court to Bromfield Streets; Gleason's Pictorial, *July 30, 1853, showing Boston Museum, King's Chapel, and Tremont Temple*

Symphony Hall

TREMONT TEMPLE.　　　　MONTGOMERY PLACE.　GLEASON'S PUBLISHING HALL.　BROMFIELD STRE

the era, was erected near Symphony Hall by Eben Jordan, at his own expense. This fine brick-and-stone building with its pilastered façade was equipped with a marquee over the carriage entrance to shelter the handsomely gowned audience as they arrived and departed in inclement weather. The rich crimson-and-gold interior provided an appropriate background for gala occasions. The first tier of boxes above the orchestra seats, known as "the diamond horseshoe," glittered with the jewels of the ladies and gentlemen in full evening dress. All this is now gone. The Opera House was torn down in 1958.

In 1848 the Old Boston Museum was built on Tremont Street, between School and Court streets. This large granite building, designed by Hammatt Billings, had a symmetrical façade ornamented with iron balconies and gas jets fitted with white glass globes. The lofty interior had a columned entrance hall of three stories with a grand staircase framed in decorative iron railings. There were rooms with statues on pedestals, pictures on the walls, and stuffed birds, animals, and waxworks scenes in glass cases. This museum, first called "The Lecture Hall," also served as a theatre with a regular company of actors who presented Shakespearean plays and old comedies. Among the well-known actresses was Mrs. J. R. Vincent for whom the Vincent Club and the Vincent Memorial Hospital were named.

The famous Old Museum building had the first air-conditioning system in the country. Air, cooled in summer over ice and warmed by steam in winter, was changed every four minutes by a gas-operated engine.

The Tremont Theatre, designed by Isaiah Rogers (1800–69) and built in 1827 opposite the old Granary Burying Ground, had one of the best-known halls in the country.

Here Charles Dickens, during his second visit to Boston in 1867, gave a series of his famous readings. This was the event of the season and tickets were in great demand. For one of these readings, presented at Christmastime, the hall was elaborately decorated with red-berried holly and festoons of greens draped over the looking glass and picture frames. The aging Dickens stood erect in front of the gas footlights, with a nosegay in the buttonhole of his lapel, fascinating his audience.

In 1838 a spacious hall on Tremont Street became the new location of Lorenzo Papanti's famous dancing school. This elegant dancing hall had French mirrors between the twelve high windows and was lighted by crystal chandeliers imported from Paris at a cost of $1,200. The most exclusive dancing classes and assemblies were held here for sixty years until the school closed in 1899. A fashionable ball and supper, which included the great American delicacy, oysters, as well as champagne, was held at Papanti's Hall for Charles Dickens. An elaborate banquet of twelve courses was also given here in 1868 in his honor, which lasted three hours.

The Boston Theatre, built in 1854 on Washington Street near Boylston Street, was the largest theatre in New England. The elegant interior had a dress circle, a family circle, and a horseshoe-shaped gallery in front of the stage. Operas were given, and a stock company produced plays here. The price of the tickets ranged from twenty-five cents to $1.50. Like the Opera House in Paris, the orchestra seats could be floored over to produce a grand ballroom. Here some of the most select balls in Boston took place, including one for the Grand Duke Alexis, one for Charles Dickens (at which the tickets were $40.00 each), and one in 1860 for the Prince of Wales, later King Edward VII of England. This was a gala evening

The Prince of Wales, 1860. (Right) Paris gown worn at the ball for the Prince, 1860

for the nineteen-year-old prince, who remained until after four in the morning. His dance card was filled in with the names of seventeen of Boston's most prominent young ladies. Three thousand guests attended. The hall was lavishly decorated with flowers and a large painting of Windsor Castle. The three tiers of boxes fitted with crimson curtains were framed with evergreens.

The ladies were lovely to look at and beautifully dressed. Many sent to Worth in Paris for the ball gowns they wore on this great occasion, and one of these may be seen today in the collection of the Museum of Fine Arts. Another of these gowns was described in *Sketches of Boston*, a pamphlet put out by L. P. Hollander Company, Inc., one of the exclusive Boston shops established in 1886. "This dress was an exact fac-simile of one worn by the Empress Eugénie on a recent occasion. Miss Brutt had a very elegant bouquet of New York manufacture, from the floral depot of Chevalier and Brower, 523 Broadway, under the St. Nicholas Hotel. It represented an imperial star and was composed of blush rose-buds, tuber roses, heartsease, acanthus leaves, and sweet alyssum. It was supported by a silver holder ornamented with deep white silk fringe." All this luxury and beauty combined to create lasting memories of this elegant ball and the magnificent building. When it was torn down in 1926 a wooden two-story house was found intact under the grand staircase to everyone's surprise.

The Howard Athenaeum * was a well-known and once first-class theater. Formerly the wooden Miller Tabernacle, it was rebuilt in 1846 by Isaiah Rogers (1800–69) in the Gothic style of granite. The richly decorated interior was

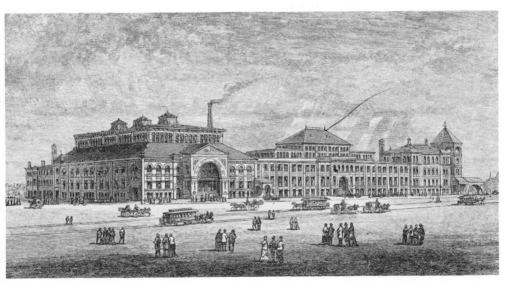

The Massachusetts Charitable Mechanics' Association Building on Huntington Avenue (demolished). From King's Hand Book of Boston *5th edition, 1883*

73

The Howard Athenaeum, 1846 (demolished)

furnished with the first cushioned theater seats in Boston. It continued as a fashionable playhouse where the opera and drama were presented until about 1870 when it became a vaudeville theater. John L. Sullivan, the pugilist from Roxbury, was then a favorite performer. After that "burlesque" was staged here, and as the Scollay Square area declined, the *Old Howard* deteriorated. This celebrated old theater was demolished in 1962.

74

One of the last of the ornate Victorian playhouses, the *Colonial Theatre* **, opened its doors in 1900. A grand foyer with a painted ceiling, marble walls, and mosaic pavement led to the box office. Ticket purchasers were kept in line by a heavy railing of polished brass. The great baroque interior glittered with gold and brightly lighted chandeliers were reflected in huge plate-glass mirrors. Tiers of boxes and balconies encircled the stage and rose high above the orchestra seated in gilt bentwood chairs in the pit. This elegant décor, in the manner of the palaces of Europe, has been recently restored to all its glory.

Horticulture

There was a growing interest in horticulture in the nineteenth century. The Massachusetts Horticultural Society, incorporated in 1829, is one of the oldest in the country. Exhibitions of flowers, fruits, and vegetables have been held from its beginning and continue now as the Horticultural Society Shows.

After two earlier buildings were torn down, the Society moved uptown to its present location at the corner of Massachusetts and Huntington avenues. This fine brick structure in the Renaissance style, with a richly carved stone frieze of swags of fruit and flowers alternating with medallions of marble, now contains the exhibition halls and the library, one of the most valuable collections of its kind.

The Mount Auburn Cemetery in Cambridge was established by the Horticultural Society in 1831 on a pleasant wooded hill known as Sweet Auburn. It was the first garden cemetery. The idea of graves under churches and in crowded

Horticultural Hall, Massachusetts Avenue

Horticultural Hall, Tremont Street, (demolished)

churchyards was considered unsuitable by Dr. Jacob Bigelow, who was instrumental in having this burial ground laid out. It remains today the tree-shaded and beautifully landscaped resting place of many famous Bostonians including Charles Bulfinch.

The Arnold Arboretum, an outstanding center of horticulture situated on the Parkway in Jamaica Plain, grew out of a gift to Harvard University from Benjamin Bussey in 1870. He gave his estate of three hundred and sixty acres as a site for a school of horticulture. It was named for James Arnold, a friend of Emerson, who contributed $100,000 for the creation of an arboretum. This famous collection of living trees and shrubs, the largest in the world, ranks in importance with Kew Gardens in England.

The Public Garden

In 1837 Horace Gray conceived the idea of a public botanical garden based on those of Europe. Near the corner of Charles and Beacon streets an immense conservatory was built for plants and birds. This housed a large and well-known collection of beautiful camellias, as well as European and tropical singing birds, and was a great attraction until it burned the following year.

The marshland beyond the west side of the Common, now Charles Street, was covered by the waters of the Back Bay at high tide. In 1850 these marshes were filled in to become the Public Garden, a pleasure ground of twenty-four acres.

Bird's-eye view of Boston, 1850, by J. Bachman, showing at left trains, bridge, Bunker Hill Monument, Beacon Hill, and the State House: The waters of the Back Bay in the foreground. Beyond, in center, the Public Garden, The Common, and the harbor

Camellia Conservatory, The Public Garden (demolished)

The swan boats, Public Garden. (Right) The equestrian statue of George Washington, Public Garden

The original plans were based on the gardens at Versailles with walks, grass plots, flower beds, trees, and a fountain. The first bed of tulips in the United States was planted here, a gift of Mr. Gray, who paid $1,500 to import the bulbs. Tulip time in the Garden is still one of the most beautiful and colorful experiences of a Boston spring season.

Later this design was changed and a four-acre pond with a miniature island was made. In 1877 rowboats and the famous *swan boats* ** were added to this lake. The latter are long barges with horizontal rows of seats and a large figure of a swan at the stern in which a man sits and propels the craft bicycle fashion. They were designed by Robert Paget and have been operated by the Paget family for three generations.

In winter, when the pond was frozen, it became a popular skating rink for old and young alike as it is today. In summer Victorian flower beds in the Garden were colorful with a profusion of dahlias, pansies, heliotrope, and cannas. These and an abundance of small-foliage plants were brought from the city hothouses, along with palms in green wooden tubs, and arranged along the walks. Several varieties of ornamental trees were planted and wooden benches were placed in their shade. Here generations of young Bostonians have played under the watchful eye of their nursemaids.

The Public Garden was enclosed by a high iron railing with elaborate entrance gates characteristic of the Victorian period.

The first equestrian statue in Boston was placed inside the Commonwealth Avenue gate in 1869. This familiar rendering of George Washington mounted on his horse by the well-known sculptor, Thomas Ball (1819–1911), was considered the finest in New England. The model for the horse was Black Prince, the mount of the Prince of Wales when he reviewed the troops on the Common in 1860.

Many other splendid memorial statues and monuments were placed in the Public Garden, along the Commonwealth Avenue Mall, and in other squares and parks in Boston during this period.

The Common

Boston Common changed little during the eighteenth century. It remained rustic and cows were pastured there until 1830, when it was made into a park. Malls were laid out on the Beacon, Park, and Tremont street sides and a little later on the Charles and Boylston street ends. These tree-shaded

The Great Elm, Boston Common. (Right) The Apple Woman,
Boston Common

paths became popular promenades and courting walks. In 1836 the old wooden pasture fences were removed and footpaths traversed the Common. The Long Path, which descends from Joy Street to the corner of Boylston and Tremont streets, is the most famous. Here the autocrat took the schoolmistress on a stroll that ended in their long walk through life together as Mr. and Mrs. Oliver Wendell Holmes.

In the Victorian period the paths were straightened and some were paved with brick. Many beautiful elms and other trees of a variety of species were planted to shade the grassy areas and benches. ‡ Along the walks old women sat under the trees and sold fruits and nuts from small carts. As in Paris, the apple woman was a favorite with the children.

The Frog Pond was surrounded by a stone curb in 1824. It became a French-style park basin in contrast to its earlier use as a watering place for cattle. It also was the site of an outstanding event in Boston.

*View of the Water Celebration, 1848, Boston Common, by
B. F. Smith, Jr.; lithographed by Tappan and Bradford*

In 1848 water was brought to the city from Lake Co-
chituate twenty miles away. Bostonians were no longer de-
pendent on wells and cisterns but had water brought directly
to their homes via a brick aqueduct, stone tunnel, and iron
pipes. This great engineering feat was celebrated by the firing
of one hundred guns at sunrise and the ringing of church
bells. This was followed later in the day by a procession to
the Common where addresses were delivered and school
children sang an *Ode on Water* written by James Russell
Lowell. Mayor Josiah Quincy, Jr., turned on the water,
which gushed up in the Frog Pond in a jet eighty feet high.
The imposing display ended with fireworks in the evening.

The magnificent Brewer Fountain added beauty and
continental charm to the Common. A gift to the city from
Gardner Brewer, it is a copy of one designed by Lienard and
given to the city of Paris in 1868. The original was awarded

The Brewer Fountain, Boston Common

the gold medal at the Paris Exhibition in 1855. Now almost concealed by the subway kiosks, it may still be seen opposite R. H. Stearns Company on the Tremont Street side.

The forty-eight acres of the common ground were enclosed by an iron fence (partially demolished in a World War II drive for scrap iron) with elaborate entrance gates set in posts of stone, and walk stiles of iron or stone. A deer park, so popular at this time, was fenced in on the Boylston Street side and a herd of deer installed. Nearby, along Charles Street, was a parade ground where the militia drilled.

There was also a bandstand on the Common where the city presented open-air band concerts on summer evenings. This was replaced in 1916 by the present Parkman bandstand.

Carting away the snow, Boston Common. (Right) Coasting down Flagstaff Hill, Boston Common, from King's Hand Book of Boston, *1883*

84

Civil War Army and Navy Monument, Boston Common. (Right)
The Shaw Memorial, Boston, by Auguste St. Gaudens

Monuments

Boston Common, so full of historic interest, added yet another chapter during the Civil War. Here the troops were mobilized in 1861 and mustered out in 1865.

The Army and Navy Monument, ** with sculpture by Martin Milmore, was erected on Flagstaff Hill in honor of the soldiers and sailors who gave their lives in this war.

The Shaw Memorial, * a large and beautiful bronze plaque opposite the entrance to the State House, is the work of the most noted American sculptor of the period, Augustus Saint-Gaudens (1848–1907). The bas-relief panel portrays Boston's Colonel Robert Gould Shaw leading his Negro regi-

85

ment, the first from Massachusetts to fight against slavery. This distinguished young gentleman, a member of one of Boston's first families, died in an attack on Fort Wagner, South Carolina, in 1863, and was buried there with his men who fell in the battle.

Outstanding among the many other Civil War monuments erected in greater Boston is the Emancipation Group * in Park Square, given to the city by Moses Kimball in 1877. The superb bronze figures of Abraham Lincoln and a kneeling slave, mounted on a granite pedestal with urns for flowers at the four corners, is the work of Thomas Ball, and a copy of the one given by freed men to the city of Washington, D. C. See illustration on page 38.

The Great Boston Fire

The great Boston fire of November 6, 1872, started in a wooden elevator shaft and burned through Saturday night until Sunday noon, destroying sixty-five acres of buildings in the area bounded by the present Summer, Washington, Milk, and Broad streets. The fire engines were handicapped by lack of horses, due to an epidemic that incapacitated most of these animals. The gas was cut off, leaving the city in darkness, and buildings were blown up in an attempt to halt the flames, but still the fire raged. Thousands lost their property or their livelihood. Seven hundred and sixty-six buildings, of which sixty-seven were of brick or stone, were rapidly consumed. The demolished Fort Hill area formed an open space which acted as a stopgap in that section. The fire finally was halted near the old State House. **

86

Ruins of the Great Boston Fire, 1872, with the Old South Church at the left. (Right) Ruins and fire engine, the Great Boston Fire, 1872

Militia guarding the ruins. (Right) Ruins of the Great Boston Fire, 1872, showing the City Hall and the steeple of the Old South Church

The Old South Church ** was saved by water played through one thousand feet of hose from the harbor. The militia was called to duty and the famous old colonial landmark was used as their barracks. After the disastrous fire this church ceased to be used for worship but has been preserved as a historic site. †

On the vast ruin was built a new district of Boston, no longer residential, as in the eighteenth and nineteenth centuries, but a great shopping and business center. These large Victorian buildings included many ornate dry-goods and other retail stores of picturesque styles. They were joined together in blocks along the newly straightened and widened streets.

It was thought that fires could not cross these broad thoroughfares or destroy these stone buildings, but within a few months other fires razed more property. Some who were burned out in the great fire lost everything again in the fires of 1873, 1874, and 1878.

The Boston Fire Department acquired more up-to-date apparatus as a result of these dreadful conflagrations. Twenty-nine steam fire engines, each with a hose carriage inscribed with its name, as well as seven chemical engines, twelve hook-and-ladder carriages, and an aerial ladder were purchased. The department also had one hundred and fifty horses and about seventy thousand feet of hose. In the days before the advent of fire engines that could be fed by water from a hydrant "hand pumpers" were used. Exhibitions, known as "the firemen's muster," drew crowds who came to see which group could "squirt the hose" the greatest distance.

Fire stations were built and, like most of the new buildings of this time, were a revival of some earlier European style. One of the finest of these remains in the South End on Bristol Street near Dover Street, and may be seen from the

The Bristol Street Fire Station. (Right) Firemen and the John S. Damrell Fire Engine #11 used in Great Boston Fire of 1872

new expressway. The picturesque building of yellow Victorian brick has a tall, square, crenelated bell tower, in the manner of an Italian campanile, which still accents the Boston skyline. From this great height fire hoses were draped through the open and shut battlements, and hung to the ground to dry out. There were Venetian balconies from which the "rookie" firemen practiced sliding down ropes. These are examples of decorative features which, though seemingly inappropriate, were functional.

Inside the building a large brass sliding pole was installed down which the firemen descended quickly from their rooms to the apparatus below. Swinging harnesses for the horses, signal boxes, and later an electric gong were among the improvements. The powerful fire horses, dashing down the street with their gleaming fire engines, were a thrilling sight. Often harnessed three abreast, they galloped over the granite cobblestones, with the bell clanging. "The three grays" from the Haymarket Square Station were one of the most celebrated of these crack teams.

Samuel Thaxter's Trade Card, showing his shop at 125 State Street

Union Bank Building, 40 State Street

Business Buildings

After the great fire of 1872 a number of fine commercial structures were built in Boston, especially in the burned-out area, which grew rapidly into a business district.

The late Victorian era brought new types of architecture and larger and more efficient buildings. The use of structural iron and the invention of the elevator, making taller buildings possible, changed the designs and methods of construction. These higher buildings were lighted by more and larger windows. Great areas of plate glass replaced the earlier small panes. The ostentation of the newly rich brought an end to the simple, classic Greek Revival style, and favored the Renaissance and picturesque Gothic types. There was a feel- of permanence, solidity, and security reflected in these massive Victorian buildings. Granite from Quincy and other parts of New England, a variety of types of local stone, and marbles imported from Italy were favorite materials. The new architecture became more and more ornate with an abundance of carved detail. As pointed out before, sculpture was in vogue. Rendered in bas-relief or in the round, it appeared on buildings and monuments. Copper was frequently used on cornices and roofs, especially on domes. This became very colorful and decorative as the metal weathered and acquired a lovely blue-green patina.

Structural iron was a basic new element and cast iron was popular for ornamental details. Large and elaborate lanterns and door grills of iron appeared on banks and other public buildings.

Interiors were made more comfortable. Furnaces provided central heating. More efficient lighting and set plumbing were installed. All these changes in buildings created a new and suitable background for the industrial age.

The State Street Block ** on the water end of State Street, opposite the Custom House, had been built in 1858 and miraculously survived the great fire. This large, symmetrical office building was among the first of Boston's massive granite mercantile structures. Designed by Gridley J. F. Bryant, it is now defaced by trade signs and the addition of upper stories, but it remains an outstanding example of the good taste of the early Victorian period. ‡

Merchants built huge office buildings, stores, and warehouses from Washington Street to the water front. A new shopping district developed in the Summer Street area and spread toward the Common, absorbing the old residential part there and along Tremont Street.

The wholesale district was another important commercial center with large office buildings in the section near Bedford, Lincoln, and Essex streets. Many of these served the leather trade. More than half of all the shoes made in the United States were manufactured in Massachusetts at this time, and the boot and shoe companies had Boston offices here.

The wool market, largest in the country, erected their office buildings in what is now the South Station area.

The fish business was also an important industry, and maintained a large fleet of fishing boats and a number of wharves and warehouses on the water front. (See illustration on page 45.)

For the most part, trade signs in the Victorian period were ugly, large, and ill-placed, defacing the buildings to which they were attached. A few were picturesque and some of these remain. The Regal Shoe Company suspended a huge boot high above the sidewalk from the front of the building

The State Street Block. (Right) The Fiske Building (1888),
State Street, one of the new palatial office buildings

The Oriental Tea Company steaming teakettle sign. (Right) The
Mutual of New York Building with tower, left, and the New
England Mutual Life Insurance Company, right (demolished)

Office of the Carter's Ink Company, 162-172 Columbus Avenue.
(Right) Interior of John Hancock Mutual Life Insurance Company
office, ca 1880

on Washington Street near the Old South Church, and the Oriental Tea Company on Court Street at Scollay Square displayed a large teakettle. * This kettle, which has a capacity of more than two hundred and twenty-seven gallons, has fascinated young and old since it was first hung out in 1874 with steam continually drifting from its great spout.

The Boston Board of Trade was organized in 1854 to bring together the businesses of the city in the interests of commerce. The Boston Chamber of Commerce was incorporated in 1885 and moved in 1890 to a beautiful new building of rough granite now occupied by the Grain and Flour Exchange. (See illustration on page 49.) This handsome edifice, with its large round turreted French Gothic tower, is a good example of the richness and solidity of the Victorian style and the influence of European architecture in Boston.

Several banking houses and insurance companies erected magnificent buildings in the State Street and Post Office Square districts. They were of stone ornamented with sculpture and ironwork in the French and Italian styles. The lofty interiors were splendid, with marble walls and floors. The equipment was up to date and included a new communication system of electric bells and speaking tubes.

Public Buildings

Victorians everywhere took great pride in their new public buildings.

One of Boston's most distinguished is the City Hall * on School Street, built in 1862. Inspired by the Tuileries and the Louvre in Paris, and designed by Gridley J. F. Bryant and Arthur Gilman, it was among the first of our French Victor-

City Hall, 1862, School Street, by Gridley J. F. Bryant; inspired by the Louvre and the Tuileries in Paris. (Below) Interior of City Hall

ian structures. The stately building of Concord granite, ornamented with coupled columns and pilasters on the façade, has a Mansart roof of wood covered with copper and slates, terminating in a Louvre-style dome which held a fire alarm. The interior woodwork is of butternut and pine. The entrance hall floor was paved with squares of black-and-white marble. The building was served by elevators, and the broad staircase was framed by iron balusters with newels and handrails of oak. The offices of all the departments necessary to run the city were here, including that of the superintendent of health, who had charge of the city stables, horses, wagons, and streetcleaners.

The Suffolk County Court House ** completed in 1889, was built to replace the Old County Court House, designed by Bulfinch in 1810, on Court Street. This immense granite

Pemberton Square looking north, 1860, showing the bow-front houses

building in the German Renaissance style was erected on the west side of Pemberton Square. The interior is still impressive. The great entrance hall, with a grand staircase and lofty rotunda, is ornamented with white marble and polished granite and adorned with sculpture and frescoes representing the human virtues.

Across the street some of the old bow-front houses remain, reminiscent of the days when this was a fashionable, tree-shaded, residential square.

The Charles Street or Suffolk County Jail, ** is another of the outstanding stone buildings of Victorian Boston. Built in 1851 from designs by Gridley J. F. Bryant in a massive octagonal shape of fine proportions, it originally had a beautiful clock tower ending in a dome topped by a weather vane.

The Old Post Office building in Post Office Square was under construction and ready for its roof when it was damaged by the great fire of 1872. It was rebuilt in the elaborate Renaissance style, with a façade rendered in Cape Ann granite and a Mansart roof of iron covered with slates. Two marble statues, representing Commerce and Industry, by Daniel Chester French (1850–1907) ornamented the Post Office Square side. The interior, once considered one of the "sights" of Boston, had a classic center hall or cash room on the second floor with walls of Siena marble slabs in light and dark shades, accented with tall pilasters of Sicilian marble and a rich frieze and cornice. A gallery or balcony ran around the four sides. In this cash room were installed the new fireproof and burglar-proof safes.

The jail on Charles Street. (Right) The old Post Office,
Post Office Square

97

The First Corps of Cadets Armory, Arlington Street at Columbus Avenue

Uptown, at the intersection of Arlington Street and Columbus Avenue, stands the rough granite First Corps of Cadets Armory. The cornerstone of this massive castellated building was laid with impressive ceremonies on October 19, 1891, the one-hundred-fiftieth anniversary of the founding of the corps. These cadets from Boston's first families had been the honorary guard for all the Massachusetts governors since 1741.

98

The building houses many outstanding military collections. Noteworthy among them is the gift of American small arms presented by General Charles Chauncey Foster (1857–1943), a rifle and pistol expert. This exhibit is one of the most complete of its kind in the United States and draws many visitors from all over the country.

The Victorian South End–More Made Land

The South Bay was filled in to form the new South End. This was not the colonial South End of the Old State House area, but the marshes and flats flanking the Neck to Roxbury. (See map on page 18.)

Worcester Square, 1851, South End. Bow front houses overlooking park

*Chester Square, South End,
showing the fountain
and the houses*

Park Square * is approximately on the spot where the old thin strip of land, known in colonial times as the Neck, joined the pear-shaped peninsula of Boston. On this Neck the only road out of town was often inundated at high tide. Earlier in the nineteenth century there had been some filling in here on the South Bay side toward Dorchester to make needed land for wharves and buildings. In 1850 the work began in earnest when the South Bay flats and marshes on the other side of the Neck toward the waters of the Back Bay were also made into land. This became the Victorian South End, * a quiet residential district of blocks of town houses.

The plan was the first large-scale layout since the English urban planning in the late eighteenth and early nineteenth centuries. The streets were so arranged that the houses overlooked green parks or squares with trees reminiscent of the great terraces of Bath and the old squares of London. It was not a hit-or-miss growth or a government-financed plan like the layouts of Paris and Washington, D.C., but was built with private capital.

The Filling-In
of The Back Bay

The filling in of the salt-water bay of the Charles River back of Boston began in 1857. The land under this water was the property of the Commonwealth of Massachusetts, and when the filling was completed this area became known as the *Back Bay*. * (See map on page 18.) It developed into a cultural and religious center as well as an elegant residential district. There were many beautiful churches, public buildings, and hotels, especially in the neighborhood of Copley Square.

The Charles River Railroad Company was of great assistance in this gigantic operation. Gravel was brought nine miles from Needham in a specially constructed train of cars pulled by a steam engine, and dumped into the waters of the Bay. The filling eliminated what had become since the construction of the mill dam an odoriferous and unhealthy body of water, and created profitable land. Streets were laid out on which lots were sold at public auction with a profit of approximately four million dollars for the state.

The street plan, based on the boulevards of Paris was designed by the architect Arthur Gilman. Commonwealth Avenue, * the main artery leading out of town from the Public Garden, was an imposing, straight street with a mall in the center. This tree-shaded walk was provided with benches and adorned with statues, including one at Dartmouth Street of William Lloyd Garrison * by Olin L. Werner. The Mall, flanked by a dual carriageway, was two hundred and forty feet wide from house to house, including twenty-foot front lawns and brick sidewalks.

*Bird's-eye view of the Back Bay and the Mill Dam showing the
waters of the Back Bay beyond Arlington Street*

Some of these grass plots were framed by railings of iron
or stone and others by a low stone curb. The small front
lawns had no planting but a few had magnolia trees planted
later. In the spring the lovely pink or white blossoms still
soften the cold dignity of the tall town houses.

The cross streets parallel to the Public Garden were
called by English names in alphabetical order. One of the
most fashionable carriage drives was around the Public Garden and along the fine new Back Bay thoroughfares past
these elegant residences.

Frederick Law Olmsted (1822–1903), the pioneer con-
servationist in the country, came to live in the Boston suburb
of Brookline in 1883. His home at 99 Warren Street was re-

cently selected as a national historic landmark. Although his best-known works are Central Park in New York City and the park at Niagara Falls, he is well known for his town planning in Boston. Beyond Massachusetts Avenue he laid out the Back Bay Fens in the eighties, which became the first parkway approach to an American city.

The landscaped roadway known as The Fenway began at the Charles River and followed the Muddy River out of town by way of Jamaica Pond and the Arnold Arboretum to Franklin Park.

Overlooking the Fenway on the corner of Boylston Street, the Massachusetts Historical Society erected its new building in 1899. This handsome Georgian Revival edifice houses the Society's superb collection of books and historical material.

The Back Bay Fens, showing Fenway Court and Simmons College

Hospitals and Charitable Homes

During the colonial period, Boston had been hostile to medical ideas and even confused them with witchcraft. Gradually the thinking changed and people began to accept Dr. Zabdiel Boylston's inoculations for smallpox in the early eighteenth century. A few young men went abroad to study medicine at that time, among them Dr. Thomas Bulfinch, father of the famous architect Charles Bulfinch.

In 1783 the Harvard Medical School was established in Cambridge largely through the efforts of Dr. John Warren. It was moved to Boston in 1816.

The Massachusetts General Hospital * received its charter in 1811 and in 1818 the first building was designed by Charles Bulfinch. ‡ Here in 1847, in the operating room under the great dome of this famous Greek Revival granite structure, ether was first administered in a surgical operation.

As Boston grew toward the important medical center it is today, more hospitals were established, many of which were in the South End. The Homeopathic Medical Dispensary, founded in 1856, became the Massachusetts Homeopathic Hospital, the largest in America.

The original buildings of the Boston City Hospital were erected on Harrison Avenue in 1864. Designed by Gridley J. F. Bryant in the French style, they overlooked a large open forecourt with a tall iron railing and gateways along the sidewalk. The administration building in the center, with its impressive dome and portico, was flanked by Mansart-roofed pavilions and formed one of the finest groups of buildings in Boston. The huge hospital, covering about seven acres, was built and supported by the city. These notable buildings have

The Boston City Hospital, South End, 1864; from
King's Hand Book of Boston, *1883*

been altered beyond recognition and concealed by later structures.

In 1865 the Carney Hospital was founded through the generosity of Andrew Carney and staffed by the Sisters of Charity. Originally situated on Dorchester Heights, South Boston, near the site where George Washington commanded the Revolutionary soldiers, it had an extensive view over the city and the harbor. This was thought to be the best situation for a hospital in New England. To quote *King's Handbook of Boston*: "In summer the hospital is cooled by the sea-breezes; and the convalescents enjoy a beautiful prospect from their beds, watching meanwhile the vessels passing in and out of the harbor."

The Children's Hospital, built on Washington Street in 1869, was equipped with sixty beds. The nursing was under the direction of the Protestant Episcopal Sisterhood of Saint Margaret, whose convent is now on the Pinckney Street corner of Louisburg Square.

The Home for Aged Men, South End, 1870, by Gridley J. F. Bryant; from King's Hand Book of Boston, *1883*

Numerous other hospitals and homes were founded in various parts of the city. This was a benevolent era, and Boston was very conscious of the needs of its less fortunate. Ladies and gentlemen alike developed an interest in merciful tasks. Busy and important men served on the boards of these institutions and gave generously to their support. A number of these organizations continue their good work today, some in their original Victorian buildings and others in larger and more efficient quarters in other parts of the city. Those were the days of individual interests in philanthropies before the Community Chest drives collected the funds.

The Home for Aged Men, established in 1861 on South Street, moved to a Mansart-roofed building at 133 West Springfield Street in 1870. This stately French Victorian structure, set in landscaped grounds and enclosed by an iron fence, had been erected in 1855 for the first lying-in hospital. Later it was used as a Civil War soldiers' home until 1869. Here in this home which he had designed Gridley J. F. Bryant was destined to spend his last days. Now known as Rogerson House, this old institution, the first in the country

106

for men, continues to serve as a home for aged men in a new location near Jamaica Pond. It is administered by a board of Boston business and professional men, some of whom are descendants of earlier directors.

The Children's Mission to the Children of the Destitute (Unitarian) was on Tremont Street, St. Vincent's Orphan Asylum for Destitute Roman Catholic Girls on Shawmut Avenue, the Boston Lunatic Hospital in South Boston, the Consumptive's Home in Roxbury, the Home for Aged Women on Revere Street, the Penitent Females' Refuge and Bethesda Society on Rutland Street, and the St. Andrew's Home for Unfortunate Scottish Immigrants on West Concord Street, were among the many types of charitable homes to mention but a few.

Although they had no building from which to administer their charity, the oldest sewing circle in Boston, *The Fragment Society*, continued their good work of "relieving the suffering poor" of the city. Founded in 1812 and named for the biblical miracle, the members still supply bedding and clothing to the needy. During the nineteenth century the Ladies' Visiting Committee called on the needy families personally to determine their wants and to bring them words of cheer. Meeting first at 17 Cornhill and subsequently in other private homes of the members, these volunteers sewed "baby suits" (now called layettes) and other required garments. "Boot orders" for new shoes were given out and are still purchased from "William H. Learnard, Boots, Shoes, and Rubbers," on Marshall Street, the oldest shoestore in Boston. Generations of prominent Boston ladies have filled the places vacated by their forebears on the board of managers. The society, steeped in tradition, carries on this and many other of its customs today.

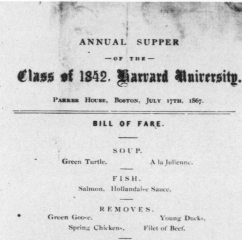

ANNUAL SUPPER
—OF THE—
Class of 1842, Harvard University.

PARKER HOUSE, BOSTON, JULY 17TH, 1867.

BILL OF FARE.

SOUP.
Green Turtle,   A la Julienne.

FISH.
Salmon, Hollandaise Sauce.

REMOVES.
Green Goose,   Young Ducks.
Spring Chickens,   Filet of Beef.

ENTREES.
Sweet Breads, au Petits Pois.
Lamb Cutlets, au Harricot Verts,   Lamb Fries, Wine Sauce.
Chicken Croquettes.

RELEVE.
ROMAN PUNCH.

GAME.
Woodcock.   Marsh Birds.

PASTRY.
Russian Charlotte.   Wine Jellies.
Biscuit Glace,   Cream Meringues.   Tipsey Cake.

DESSERT.
Grapes,   Raspberries,   Cherries.
Pine Apples,   Almonds,   Walnuts,   Raisins,   Ginger.
Ice Creams,   Orange Water Ices,
OLIVES,   COFFEE.

BILL OF FARE.

Soup.
Mock Turtle.

Fish.
Baked Tautog, Port Wine Sauce.

Removes.
Boiled Capon and Pork;
Roast Fillet of Beef, with Mushrooms;
"   Chicken;
"   Goose;
"   Ham, Champagne Sauce.

Cold Ornamental Dishes.
Galantine of Turkey, with Jelly;
Mayonnaise of Chicken;
Paté de Foie d'Oie, au Truffe.

Side Dishes.
Sweetbreads, Larded, with Green Peas;
Vol au Vent, à la Financiere;
Broiled Squabs, with Parsley;
Macaroni, à la Crème;
Fillet of Chicken, Tomato Sauce.

Game.
Woodcocks.

Glacé Pudding;   Charlotte Russe;   Madeira Jelly;   Chantilla Baskets;
Meringues à la Crème;   Confectionery.

ORNAMENTS.

Dessert.
Oranges;   Grapes;   Pineapples;   Raspberries;   Bananas;
Raisins;   Nuts;   Nectarine Ice Cream.

COFFEE AND LIQUEURS.

*Menu, Harvard Class of 1842.
Annual supper at the Parker
House, 1867*

*Part of the show set of Royal Worcester China at the
Tremont House, Boston*

Hotels and Restaurants

Boston's hotels and restaurants, which replaced the earlier inns, taverns, and coffeehouses were increasing in number and becoming famous. They offered the latest luxuries for the comfort of the guests, who enjoyed gas lights and central heating. In 1868 Charles Dickens said "Boston has the best society, best hotels, best suburbs, and the best appreciation of any city in America."

The *United States Hotel* (1826–1929) was the largest Boston hotel. It covered two acres and had five hundred rooms.

The famous *Tremont House* (1828–94) stood at the corner of Tremont and Beacon streets beside the old Granary Burying Ground **. It was the pioneer "first-class hotel" in the country. ‡

In 1847 the porticoed *Revere House* was built in Bowdoin Square and became the most comfortable and homelike of the hotels of its day. Situated in this fashionable district, opposite the Cambridge Horsecar Station, it was easily accessible and a favorite winter residence for families. Many distinguished transient guests stopped here, including Jenny Lind, the Prince of Wales, and Daniel Webster, who delivered many a speech from the iron-railed balcony.

The *Parker House* *, founded in 1854, was built on the corner of Tremont and School streets from plans by Gridley J. F. Bryant. Later there was an addition on the School Street side and here Charles Dickens stayed during his second visit to Boston in 1868, having "a parlour and little bedchamber." Harvey D. Parker, the proprietor, was one of the last in Boston to greet his guests personally on their arrival. These

The Hotel Vendome, overlooking Commonwealth Avenue

were picturesque, bustling occasions complicated by the
patron's array of hand satchels, dress suitcases, and shawls in
leather straps.

The Parker House is the only one of these early Victorian hotels still in business downtown. The food has always
been excellent and Parker House rolls have become a tradition.

At the corner of Boylston and Tremont streets, in the
present theater district, is *The Touraine*, another hotel once
famous for its décor and service. The details of the ground
floor and the one above were inspired by the châteaux of the
Touraine. The dining room, library, and ladies' parlors were
copied from rooms in these well-known châteaux and created
a fitting background for the elegant patronage of the day.

The old *Hotel Victoria*, at the corner of Newbury and
Dartmouth streets, with its Moorish detail rendered in brick,
and the recently demolished *Hotel Westminster* with a façade
abundantly decorated with large sculptured caryatids, reflected the Victorian vogue for earlier European styles.

In 1872 the *Hotel Vendome* was built at the corner of Commonwealth Avenue and Dartmouth Street from designs by William G. Preston. This palatial white-stone hotel overlooking the Mall was in the French-Victorian style. Although much altered, it is still one of Boston's most exclusive residential hotels. The original interior was spacious and decorated in the height of fashion. The great dining hall, seating three hundred and twenty, was of carved mahogany and cherrywood set with large plate-glass mirrors and adorned with frescoes and a rich frieze. The elevator was heavily paneled in wood with beveled-edged mirrors and had a built-in seat for passengers. The large-scale furniture was elaborate and the upholstery and draperies were of luxurious textiles richly trimmed with fringes and tassels. Enormous looking glasses and many large pictures graced the walls. Colossal chandeliers with the first incandescent lamps in New England illuminated all this splendor.

Boston hotels of the Victorian era were well known for their cuisine, offering a bill of fare of great variety and many courses.

These abundant meals were served from many dishes and side dishes by a corps of attentive waiters and wine stewards. Magnificence and plenty were in vogue.

There were nearly five hundred cafés and restaurants in Boston in the 1880's. Louis F. Ober's French restaurant on Winter Place offered superior viands and continues to do so today as *Lock-Ober's*. * The men's dining room on the ground floor, with its Victorian décor, leather-upholstered chairs, and long bar remains unchanged.

Jake Wirth's, serving good German food on Stuart Street since 1868, still has waiters dressed in black coats and white aprons and sawdust on the floor.

Durgin-Park's, near the Faneuil and Quincy Markets, is another old-time eating place. In this plain upstairs dining room the market men in their white coats and straw hats mingle with the other patrons and enjoy the generous portions of good food.

Clubs

For some time small intellectual groups had gathered in private homes to exchange ideas. The literary clubs of Boston grew out of these meetings. The *Saturday Club* became the most important of these. Organized in 1855, the gentlemen met at three in the afternoon once a month at the Parker House to discuss cultural subjects and to dine. A sumptuous dinner of seven courses was served with wines in a private dining room. The elected membership, composed mostly of authors and scientists, included some of the most noted men in the country.

Many other Boston clubs were established at this time and several are still active today.

The Somerset Club, said to be the oldest club in Boston, has changed its name and location several times. It started as the Travelers Club, but it was called the Tremont Club when in 1846 it met on Tremont Street. Then in 1852 it moved to the corner of Beacon and Somerset streets and took the name which it retains today. The stately old granite Sears Mansion at 42 Beacon Street ‡ has been its clubhouse since 1872.

The Union Club was formed in 1863 during the dark days of the Civil War by a group of men who believed, with

President Lincoln, that the Union should be preserved at all costs. Two of the fine old Beacon Hill houses overlooking the Common at 8 Park Street make up their clubhouse.

The St. Botolph Club (the old name for Boston or St. Botolph's Town in Lincolnshire, England) was established in 1880 at 85 Boylston Street opposite the Public Garden. This club for artists, writers, and professional men is now at 115 Commonwealth Avenue.

The Union Boat Club, one of the oldest boat clubs in the country, has existed since 1851. It is located at 144 Chestnut Street at the foot of Beacon Hill with a boathouse nearby on the Charles River for the rowing shells of the members.

The Boston Yacht Club, chartered in 1868, was the first permanent yacht club in the city. The original wooden building was on City Point. Still situated on Boston Harbor, the club is very active in a new location at 1795 Columbia Road and at their other clubhouse in Marblehead.

The Boston Yacht Club, City Point; from King's Hand Book of Boston, *1883*

The Boston Art Club, Newbury Street at Dartmouth Street; from
King's Hand Book of Boston, *1883*

The *Boston Art Club,* * at the corner of Dartmouth
and Newbury streets, now the Bryant and Stratton Commercial School, was organized in 1855. The elegant clubhouse of
brown stone and brick with Romanesque arches, rich carving
of Renaissance detail, and a hexagonal tower topped with an
onion dome of sheathed copper is typical of the taste of the
era.

In 1887 the *Algonquin Club* was built at 219 Commonwealth Avenue from designs by McKim, Mead, and White.
The fine classical building of granite still houses the club and
stands as a monument to these well-known architects of the
late Victorian period.

114

Newspapers and Magazines

Many daily and weekly newspapers were published in Boston in the nineteenth century, some of which are still in business. Telegrams and cablegrams, invented at this time, transmitted news quickly. Newspapers were printed by steam-driven machines and distributed in Newspaper Row on Washington Street. Among these were the *Herald*, the *Traveler*, the *Daily Advertiser*, the *Post*, and the *Boston Evening Transcript*. The latest news was hurriedly written on blackboards with chalk or in ink on great sheets of paper and hung outside the building. Crowds gathered to read these bulletins, especially those on political elections and sporting

The Youth's Companion Building, corner of Columbus Avenue and Berkeley Street with fine Romanesque archways and carved ornament

Bark President, *Captain Benjamin Clifford, sperm whaler*

events. In the 1880's there were nine daily newspapers printed in Boston, of which the *Daily Advertiser* was the oldest. There were also five Sunday papers and some weeklies.

The *Boston Evening Transcript*, founded in 1830, was the oldest evening paper in New England, highly regarded by conservative and intellectual people for more than a hundred years. It ceased publication in 1941.

There were many other publications in the city at this time besides those already noted. Illustrated magazines were popular, especially the home and juvenile periodicals. One of these, *The Youth's Companion*, the oldest in the country, ceased publication in 1929. This young folks' weekly had many engravings and aimed to elevate the taste of its readers.

Inventions & Scientists

In 1789 Count Rumford, who had lived in Boston, †
wrote a paper on the chemical properties attributed to light.
Later experiments along these lines on the effects of rays on
silver chloride led to the invention of photography. This
revolutionized the type of art displayed in homes and the
illustrations in newspapers, magazines, and books.

Large photographs of the Greek temples on the Acrop-
olis, the Colosseum at Rome, et cetera, under glass and,
framed in heavy dark or gilded wood were hung in school-
rooms. Religious subjects decorated the walls of Sunday
schools, and all types were popular in private homes.

Photographs, almost life-size, of just the head and shoul-
ders of former presidents and benefactors, were given a
prominent place on the walls of banks, schools, and charitable
homes, and labeled with small brass identification plaques.

Family photographs, both large and small, were found
in profusion on the walls, mantelpieces, tables, desks, and
bureaus in residences.

Following the invention of daguerreotypes in 1839 the
small-scale family pictures and other views were popular until
the end of the Civil War years. These were elaborately
framed in cases of embossed black leather lined with red plush
or satin.

The new pictorial inventions in a large measure super-
seded the fine oil portraits of earlier days.

The invention of the sewing machine by Elias Howe of
3 Cornhill changed production of garments and shoes from
handmade and homemade to "ready to wear." Retail em-
poriums and large department stores became outlets for the
goods.

The great whaling industry declined after 1859 when petroleum was discovered and kerosene replaced whale oil in lamps. Gas came into use and in turn gave way to Edison's electric light.

Communications were improving. New and astonishing discoveries changed the social and economic structure. The telegraph, the Atlantic cable, electricity, the telephone, and innumerable other miracles wrought by science changed the Victorian way of life. Of these the telephone was particularly associated with Boston.

Alexander Graham Bell (1847–1922) came from Canada in 1872 to be professor of vocal psychology at the University of Boston in their School of Oratory and to work with the children at the Boston City School for the Deaf. Although there was little interest in this field at that time, his

Wall telephone used in Boston, 1882. (Right) Women operators of the multiple switchboard, main office of the New England Telephone and Telegraph Company, 50 Pearl Street, 1886

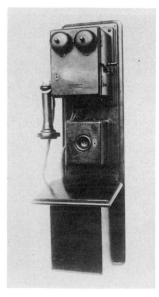

tireless labors bore fruit. In 1877 this school became the Horace Mann School for the Deaf and was free to residents of the city. Bell taught in the schools during the day and worked on his inventions at night. In 1876 he read a paper on his "Researches in Telephony" to the American Academy of Arts and Sciences in their rooms at the Boston Athenaeum. This was followed by a demonstration of the telephone. The members listened through his instruments as he played the organ nearby on Beacon Street at Boston University. Later that year, at the Centennial Exhibition in Philadelphia, his telephone received recognition by the world's most learned scientists.

Schools and Colleges

Interest in education was paramount. Schools were enlarged and new ones were established. These institutions, like the hospitals, businesses, and other groups, became so numerous that it is impossible to mention them all, but a few which still exist should be noted.

The *Chauncey Hall School* founded in 1828 on Chauncey Place, a private school for both boys and girls from kindergarten to college, moved to the Copley Square district on Boylston Street in 1873 where it remains today as a college preparatory school for boys.

Boston College, a Jesuit institution established in 1863, was housed in a red-brick building adjoining *The Church of the Immaculate Conception* at the corner of Harrison Ave-

*The New England Natural History Museum, 1864, Berkeley Street.
(Right) The Massachusetts Institute of Technology, Rogers
Building, 1866 (demolished), Boylston Street*

nue and East Concord Street. By 1883 there were sixteen
professors and instructors in the college. After forty-five
years in the South End it moved to the large Gothic buildings
at the present location in Chestnut Hill.

In 1864 *The Museum of Natural History* erected a beautiful building on Berkeley Street. The stately building of
brick and stone was designed by William G. Preston (1844–
1910) in the Renaissance style with carved heads of animals
on the keystones. With its companion, the Rogers Building,
it occupied the entire block of landscaped grounds bounded
by Berkeley, Newbury, Clarendon, and Boylston streets,
making a handsome unit. The old museum building remains
today little changed on the exterior and is carefully maintained and used as a store by the Bonwit Teller Company
since 1947. When The Natural History Museum moved to
its new building on the Charles River Dam the name of the
organization was changed to *The Museum of Science*.

The first building of *The Massachusetts Institute of
Technology* (see opposite page) was erected in 1866 on

Clarendon Street facing Boylston Street. It was designed by the same architect, William G. Preston, and named for the founder and first president, William Barton Rogers. This structure was not only a gem of architecture in the French style but was beloved by the students, especially the monumental granite front steps which were to Tech what the fence is to Yale. The first School of Architecture in the United States was established at M.I.T. and appropriately housed in the Rogers Building. Here the Lowell Lectures were given by eminent scholars. These were open free to the public, as they still are today, through the generosity of John Lowell, Jr., who left the funds for this purpose in his will of 1839. Cambridge in 1913 became the new location of *The Massachusetts Institute of Technology* where it remains today overlooking the Charles River.

The Chauncy Hall Schoolhouse, Copley Square, 1874. (Right) The New England Conservatory of Music, Franklin Square, South End

The New England Conservatory of Music was founded in 1867 and moved in 1882 into the St. James Hotel building overlooking the tree-shaded, and flower-filled Franklin Square in the South End. At this time the faculty numbered about one hundred teachers, among them some of the best musicians in Boston. Later, in 1901, it moved to its new building on Huntington Avenue where it is now located. Here the concert hall, known as Jordan Hall, was the gift of Eben D. Jordan.

The St. James Hotel then became a large nonprofit residence for working girls and students. It remains so today as the *Franklin Square House.*

The emancipation of women was furthered by other Boston educational institutions. John Simmons, a wealthy clothing merchant, was a pioneer in the field of training young women to earn a living. In 1870 he endowed *Simmons Female College* for the purpose of teaching " — medicine, music, drawing, designing, telegraphy, and other branches of art, science, and industry best calculated to enable the scholars to acquire an independent livelihood . . ." *Simmons College* is still outstanding in preparing its students for careers.

In 1873 *The Massachusetts Normal Art-School* was established by the state to train teachers to instruct in drawing. This school was set up in the old Deacon House, out on the Neck on Washington Street. In its heyday this magnificently appointed mansion was staffed with French servants. The porte-cochére is thought to have been the first in the city. Among the treasures brought from abroad for this house were eighteenth-century paintings by Fragonard and carved and gilded French paneling from the Hôtel de Montmorency in Paris. Four of these panels are now on display in the Museum of Fine Arts.

The Deacon House, South End. (Right) Carved and gilded wall panel from the Hotel Montmorency, Paris, France, installed in the Deacon Mansion. Now in the Museum of Fine Arts

The Boston Cooking School became famous through its outstanding student, Fannie Merritt Farmer, who later became director. In 1896 she published *The Boston Cooking-School Cook Book*. It was an instant success and outsold the popular novels of the day, including *Little Women*. The first edition contained household hints, such as how to clean lamps and remove stains, as well as "family" recipes and menus for twelve-course formal dinners. Miss Farmer introduced level spoon and cup measurements, which replaced the inaccurate "pinch, heaping teaspoonful, and butter the size of a walnut" method. She was also a pioneer in the science of food and at

Bird's-eye view of the Public Garden and the partially filled-in bay back of Boston. Left, the Arlington Street Church (Unitarian), 1861

one time conducted a course in nutrition at the Harvard Medical School. Her school, known as *Miss Farmer's School of Cookery*, was founded in 1902, and continues to be a Boston institution. It is now coeducational and prepares its students to be chefs and dietitians as well as cooks in the home. Her book, still in print, has outsold all other cookbooks for more than sixty years.

Little, Brown and Company, publishers of the Fannie Farmer cookbook and many other important books by local authors, completed in 1962 its one hundred and twenty-fifth year of bookmaking in Boston.

Churches

Victorian church buildings in the city were mostly large stone revivals of earlier European styles. These were very different from the earlier meetinghouses and churches in the old part of Boston. (See *Book of Boston, Colonial Period*, and *Book of Boston, Federal Period*.) The Back Bay and the new South End had many of these places of worship serving the many new and old denominations. There is room to mention only a few.

The Arlington Street Church (Unitarian) ** was the first church erected in the Back Bay. Built in 1861, at the corner of Arlington and Boylston streets, it was occupied by the congregation from the Federal Street Church where William Ellery Channing had been the minister.

Designed by Gridley J. F. Bryant and Arthur Gilman in the manner of James Gibb's London churches, the Arlington Street Church was built of the brownstone so popular in the Victorian period. There was a beautiful balustrade with large urns, now mostly removed due to the deterioration of the soft stone. A tall clock tower terminated in a graceful spire. This handsome brownstone edifice set the fashion for brownstone houses in the Back Bay. The lofty interior with its great coffered, barrel-vaulted ceiling supported by majestic Corinthian columns is painted white. The dark oak pulpit and railing are by Henry Hobson Richardson. The arched windows were fitted with inside slat blinds and small clear glass panes, but later some were replaced with Tiffany glass. Such pictorial memorial panels of this American glass were rare, and few still exist.

Left, Church of the Covenant (Presbyterian-Congregational), 1867, designed by Richard M. Upjohn, and Emmanuel Church (Episcopal) 1862, on the right, Newbury Street

The First Church of Boston (Unitarian), 1868, Berkeley Street.
(Right) The First Baptist Church, 1873, Clarendon Street and Commonwealth Avenue, by Henry Hobson Richardson, with a carved frieze and trumpeting angels on the tower, by Bartholdi, the sculptor of the Statue of Liberty

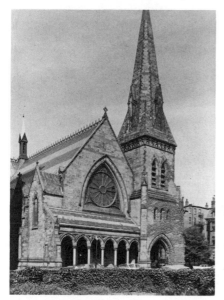

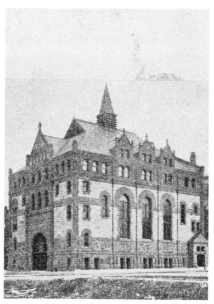

The Cathedral of the Holy Cross (Catholic), 1875, South End.
(Right) The first Spiritual Temple, now the Exeter Street Theatre; from Recent Church Architecture in Boston by A. R. Willard, New England Magazine, February, 1890

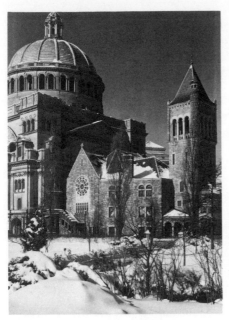

Right, The First Church of Christ Scientist, 1893; left, the larger extension. (Right) The new Old South Church (Congregational), 1877, Copley Square

Overlooking Copley Square, named for the well-known colonial painter John Singleton Copley, stands one of the finest church buildings in the country. Trinity Church (Episcopal) ** , designed by the eminent architect Henry Hobson Richardson (1838–88), was begun in 1874 and finished in 1877. Two promising young architects, Charles Follen McKim and Stanford White, worked with him on the drawings. Twenty years later the porch and triple entrances along with the tops of the western towers were added by Shepley, Rutan, and Coolidge.

The beloved rector, Phillips Brooks, was instrumental in moving the parish to the Back Bay and securing his friend Richardson as the architect for the new church building. This massive masonry structure, in the French Romanesque style of the eleventh century with cloisters and a chapel, was Rich-

128

ardson's masterpiece. It was well planned to be viewed from four sides and to fit into a triangular plot facing an important avenue.

The church was raised on forty-five hundred wooden piles driven into the water below the made land. These supports must be kept wet to avoid rotting and to secure the building. For this purpose a small boat was kept in the water under the church and when it touched bottom more water was pumped into the area. This has now been replaced by an automatically controlled system, but the huge stone structure, terminating in a great tower weighing nearly nineteen million pounds, is still supported on these piers.

Trinity Church (Episcopal), 1874, Copley Square, by Henry Hobson Richardson, showing the Bristol Hotel Apartments, the Rogers Building, and the Natural History Museum at the left

*Henry Hobson Richardson. (Right) Statue of Phillips Brooks,
by St. Gaudens*

The different kinds of stone used in the church were brought from several localities. The freestone for the trimmings came from Longmeadow, the granite from Rockport, Quincy, and Maine. The red granite and most of the foundation stone were retrieved from the earlier church on Summer Street which had burned in the great fire of 1872.

The spacious interior is rich with polychrome and gold decorations designed and executed by John LaFarge (1835–1910) of New York, in cooperation with Augustus Saint-Gaudens (1846–1907). The windows on the west and north sides, one of which was given in memory of McKim's wife, were by LaFarge. The English windows on the south are by William Morris (1834–96) with the figures by Sir Edward Burne-Jones (1833–98).

In 1891 Phillips Brooks was elected the sixth Episcopal bishop of Massachusetts. A full-length statue of him in his bishop's robes by Augustus Saint-Gaudens stands on the Boylston Street side of the church. He is warmly remembered as a distinguished religious leader and as the author of the Christmas carol, "O Little Town of Bethlehem."

130

Residences

During the early years of the Victorian period Boston homes changed little from the conservative Greek Revival style. These were uniform rows of tall bow-front town houses with large windows and classic iron balconies. They were frequently built around tree-shaded parks enclosed by castiron railings and adorned with one or two iron pedestal fountains. The twin squares, Franklin and Blackstone, which developed from Bulfinch's Columbia Square ‡ on the old Neck, are the largest. Like the others, they were framed by a carriageway, brick sidewalks with granite curbs, and tall street lights of iron lit by gas. Several of these lovely old

Union Park, South End, bow-front houses

Belmont *(demolished)*, *a great classical country house set in extensive landscaped grounds*

The Amos E. Adams house, 1888, Newton; suburban estate

squares survive in the South End, among them Franklin, * Blackstone, * Worcester, * and Union Park * with their fine houses now in regrettable condition. Beacon Hill had two of these picturesque retreats, Pemberton and Louisburg squares. The latter remains residential and little changed on the exterior today.

The last of the large classical country houses in greater Boston were built during this period. These include the Forbes house on Milton Hill and the Cushing-Payson house in Belmont. This house called *Belmont,* for which the present suburb was named, was an outstanding example. While existing contracts show that Asher Benjamin was connected with *Belmont,* Mr. Cushing's diary mentions that a number of other architects were consulted. Built of brick painted yellow, this fine classical house had a formal interior with round rooms, an oval music room, double parlors, and a stair well lit by a skylight of stained glass. The spacious grounds of about two hundred acres were laid out with avenues bordered with oak, walnut, and magnolia trees. There was a large conservatory and fourteen greenhouses devoted to the growing of fruits, plants, and vegetables. The south lawn of twenty acres was shaded by fine purple beeches. There was also a deer park on the estate. This important Greek Revival house with its lavish Victorian landscaping, finished in 1837, was demolished in 1927. Two rooms exist and are now the property of the Society for the Preservation of New England Antiquities.

The great country seats with their classical bow-front mansions were succeeded by large, picturesque Victorian suburban houses with many gables and verandas. Some residences in this style were built on street lots in Boston and the vicinity. As the city became crowded, others were built farther out of town set in tree-shaded grounds with long, winding driveways leading to the residence and stables. Conservatories were often attached to these houses. Separate greenhouses with a Victorian curved roof, provided flowers, ferns, plants, and fruit. Successful Boston businessmen built these homes in the new suburbs within an easy carriage drive of the city. A few still remain in Brookline, Longwood, Jamaica Plain, Chestnut Hill, and Milton. In later years many of these extensive Victorian estates have been subdivided to provide suburban streets and house lots.

Town houses, too, reflected this era of private luxury and the gradual disappearance of simplicity. Boston became a city of bay windows. (See illustration on page 25.) Rows of ornate brick-and-brownstone, single-family dwellings lined the city's streets, especially in the Back Bay.

Just after the Civil War the South End was in its heyday. Many of the blocks of attached town houses were of uniform design with bow fronts, but others had straight fronts with angular bay windows and some were twin houses. All had high front steps with decorative railings and a small lawn enclosed by a stone curb and a fence. The houses were generally of three stories with dormer windows lighting the attic and large windows in the full basement. There was a service entrance on an alley in the rear used for deliveries.

The interior plan varied little. The rooms opened off a long, narrow hallway. The drawing room and library were on the second floor with the chambers and one bathroom above. The basement kitchen was below the ground-floor dining room serviced by a dumb-waiter and several pantries. (May be seen at the Gibson House Museum.)

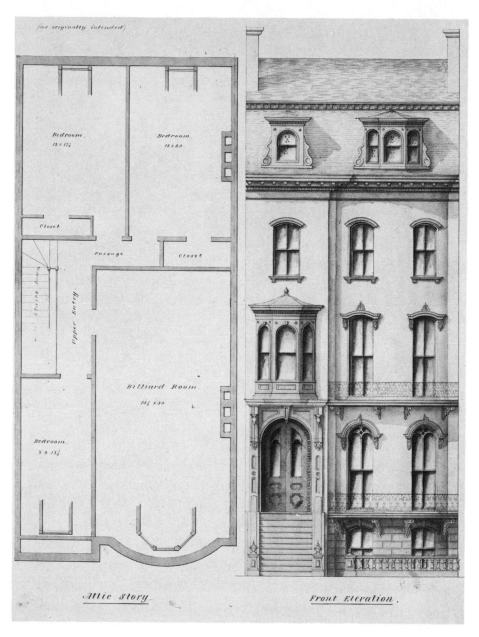

The Wallis residence, 1858, Chester Square, South End,
by L. Briggs, Jr., showing the attic story room plan

Parlor in the Josiah Quincy House, Park Street,
overlooking the Common

These town houses were dignified homes. They had high ceilings and large rooms lighted by tall windows set with large panes of plate glass in each sash. To soften the light and insure privacy they were hung with dark roller shades, glass curtains of net or lace, and framed with heavy, richly trimmed overdraperies. The rooms were crowded with possessions, some of which were beautiful and luxurious. The furniture was substantial and comfortable. Marble-top tables were popular. "Sets" were the fashion. The parlor or drawing room, dining room, and bedrooms had many of these matching pieces. The most elegant reception and drawing rooms were

136

furnished with French gilt sets, others had rosewood or walnut sofas and chairs with rich coverings of brocade, tapestry, velvet, damask, or plush protected by antimacassars. Later in the period black haircloth was popular, and overstuffed furniture was Turkish tufted and buttoned, and finished with deep fringe around the bottom. Bedroom upholstery was of cretonne, linen, or "watered silk." There were figured carpets, huge chandeliers, and enormous French plate-glass mirrors. Flowered carpets and textiles reflected the interest in flower gardens at this time.

The rooms had many accessories. Mantelpieces, draped with a cloth lambrequin, were crowded with a collection of ornaments including pictures, vases, candelabra, a clock or "timepiece," with many photographs beside it. Collections were displayed on whatnots. Pedestals held statues, usually a copy of a classic figure or bust in marble, bronze, or plaster. Tables with long fringed cloths were piled high with books, albums, a tall vase of flowers, a "rose jar" of dried petals, a humidor for cigars, and other novelties. The center table, encircled by chairs, held a reading lamp. Rogers groups were very popular, and almost everyone had one of these casts of sculptured groups of figures in attitudes of everyday life. House plants, especially Boston ferns, palms, and rubber plants, were in vogue. These were set in elaborate jardinieres of all sizes and types on tables and on the floor. The interest in birds and bird watching was stimulated by the prints of John James Audubon (1780–1851). The newly established natural-history collections were reflected in the homes. Stuffed birds, frequently ·owls, perched on bookcases or mantelpieces. The heads of animals, especially the bear and the antlered buck, were attached to the walls. Quantities of bric-a-brac, ornate silver, china, and glass, including cut glass,

Dining room in the James M. Beebe house, 1863, 30 Beacon Street

Bohemian, and Tiffany, were among the treasured possessions. Numerous water colors, prints, steel engravings, and oil paintings were hung on the walls. Currier and Ives prints were popular, inexpensive pictures. Few took time to study or become connoisseurs and great collectors, but all acquired the popular "works of art." Copies of famous paintings and antique sculpture of all sizes were a must. People were traveling more. Many of these were brought from abroad when the family took the grand tour. Genre, or storytelling pictures, peaceful landscapes, vigorous seascapes, and realistic renderings of animals, still life, fruit, and flowers were eagerly purchased and given a prominent place in the home.

The French Flats, *308-310 Commonwealth Avenue, showing double bow fronts, Byzantine carving, and Romanesque doorway*

A new form of housing, apartments known as "French Flats," was built in the South End and the Back Bay. These massive, bay-windowed, six-story buildings had ten rooms, all on one floor, opening off one side of a long corridor. These apartments, with few exceptions, are now cut up into small suites of rooms.

Although the Back Bay never had the unity in its architecture or the superior layout of the South End, it became a fashionable place to live and the "elite" moved there. How-

The Bartlet house, 172 Commonwealth Avenue. (Right) French château-style mansion, corner of Fairfield Street and Commonwealth Avenue

ever, it did not build up quickly, perhaps due to the Civil War. For years there were many vacant lots between the houses. Hit-or-miss building and a great variety of size, material, and detail contributed to the lack of harmony in the Back Bay.

The houses were generally attached, even the large mansions. Some were designed as twin residences, and there were a few groups of tall, narrow, uniform, or identical houses in each block. The bay-windowed façades had the French-style double doors in the entrance, each with a large Victorian pane of glass. All had high front steps. (See illustration on page 25.) Many were embellished with woodbine, wistaria, or Boston ivy.

Most of the houses in the Back Bay were of brick or brownstone with a French roof of either the steep-pitched

140

The residence of Mrs. Edwin S. Webster, 306 Dartmouth Street, overlooking Commonwealth Avenue, a French Victorian mansion with a conservatory at the left

or the Mansart style. Still standing and noteworthy among these is the Webster mansion at 306 Dartmouth Street, designed by the architect J. H. Sturgis in 1872, and 163 Marlborough Street, known as the Cushing-Endicott House.

Late in the period there were some outstanding classical houses with smooth façades of dressed stone. The handsome bow-front granite mansion at 303 Commonwealth Avenue is one of these. Designed by McKim, Mead, and White in 1895, it is considered their best domestic building in Boston.

The later Victorians preferred a combination of materials and styles in their architecture to the restful symmetry of the earlier Classic Revival or the uniformity of the earlier South End blocks.

Some Back Bay houses were magnificent, others reflected the taste of the times and the beginning of the decline to

The Herbert Sears house, 1893, 287 Commonwealth Avenue, a late classical Victorian mansion by McKim, Mead, and White

follow. A few were built for speculation, and these were usually smaller and plainer. The large mansions were pseudo French châteaus and Italian palaces with many rooms requiring many servants to maintain them. It was not uncommon to have ten or twelve servants, including three or four men. There were uniformed cooks, butlers, a coachman, a houseman, a governess, a second scullery, chamber, parlor, lady's, and nursemaids.

The interior plan of the Back Bay houses varied little from the town houses of the South End with the exception that there were often more stories.

*The Andrew house, 1884, by McKim, Mead, and White, with the
Marie Antoinette balcony brought from Paris*

Bedchamber in the Brewer house, 29 Beacon Street

The family rooms in these houses were elegantly decorated and often had silk, tapestry, frescoes, or rich papers on the walls. The large, elaborately ornamented furniture was combined with inherited pieces of earlier periods and with family portraits. These interiors, even though usually luxurious, were typically Victorian, with a cluttered accumulation of good and bad.

144

Upstairs sitting room in the Gibson House, 137 Beacon Street.
(Right) Dining room in the Gibson House, 137 Beacon Street.

At 137 Beacon Street ** Mrs. Charles Hammond Gibson built a town house which became the winter home of this family for three generations. Her grandson endowed and left it as a museum open free to the public. Completely furnished as it was lived in, it is a fine example of a Victorian Boston home.

This house, built in 1859, one of the first built in the Back Bay, is now more than one hundred years old. It is a twin to the adjoining Russell house at 135 Beacon Street, which was erected at the same time. Both are of brownstone and brick with a central entrance doorway fitted with double doors in the French manner and approached by the usual high flight of stone steps. Above the front door a characteristic

Music room in the Gibson House, 1858, 137 Beacon Street

"Bamboo" bedroom furniture in the Gibson House, 137 Beacon Street

angular bay window not only admits more light, but also affords a pleasant place to sit and look up and down the street.

The interior has the characteristic heavy dark woodwork and red-carpeted stairs leading to the drawing room above. An immense open stair well continues to the top of the house. From the basement kitchen to the maids' rooms there are six floors and no elevator.

Entrance hall and front stairs in the Gibson House,
137 Beacon Street

*Portrait of Mrs. John Low-
ell Gardner, Jr., 1888, by
John Singer Sargent
(1856–1925)*

Mr. and Mrs. John Lowell Gardner, Jr., lived at 152
Beacon Street, on the water side, in a French Victorian
brownstone house built by Mrs. Gardner's father for her when
she came to Boston as a bride. Here the stylish little yellow
drawing room was a bit of Paris in Boston. During the years
she was acquiring her superb art collection she lived here and
abroad.

After Mr. Gardner's death in 1899 she built *Fenway
Court,* ** the magnificent combination residence and museum
where she spent her last years. This home, known as "Mrs.
Jack Gardner's Palace," was inspired by the palaces she knew
so well in Venice. In her day it was the scene of many excellent concerts and stately receptions.

The courtyard was filled with flowers, and the rare paintings and other treasures of this priceless private collection were displayed in the rooms surrounding it. Open to the public as *The Isabella Stewart Gardner Museum*, it now affords an opportunity for all to enjoy beautiful music, flowers, and works of art.

Courtyard of Fenway Court, home of Mrs. John Lowell Gardner, Jr.

The old Museum of Fine Arts, 1876, Copley Square

Museums

The Museum of Fine Arts, incorporated in 1870, received many loans and gifts from Boston families who have thus permanently enriched the city. In 1876 the first building was erected in Copley Square to house and exhibit these treasures and other important collections. Designed by Sturgis and Brigham, it stood on the site of the present Sheraton Plaza Hotel. It was not so distinguished as the other buildings surrounding the Square. As Thomas E. Tallmadge describes it in his *Story of Architecture in America*, "an English building with Italian detail and hardly enough mistakes to make it entirely American." This large, gabled brick edifice, with Gothic-style arches and polished marble columns topped with red and buff-colored terra-cotta capitals, was unique.

The interior was spacious. Broad iron staircases led to the upper galleries where a variety of fine collections were displayed in the exhibition rooms. By 1909 the museum had outgrown this building and moved to the present handsome edifice on Huntington Avenue designed by Guy Lowell.

The Boston Athenaeum, Ballou's Pictorial, *wood engraving by Henry Bricker after a drawing by Asa Warren*

Panorama of Copley Square showing Trinity Church, Museum of

Libraries

Boston is a city of many libraries, both private and public. The Boston Library Society, founded in 1794, was first housed in the lower rooms over the arch in the Tontine Crescent building ‡ on Franklin Street, which had been donated to them by Charles Bulfinch. Later it became part of the *Boston Athenaeum* collection.

This distinguished private library, incorporated in 1807, moved to 10½ Beacon Street. The stately brown sandstone Italian Renaissance-style edifice, designed by Edward C. Cabot, stands back from the street with a stone balustrade along the sidewalk. The interior with floors of lofty book-lined rooms, paintings, and sculpture overlooks the old Gran-

Fine Arts, S. S. Pierce Company, and the Public Library

ary Burying Ground and the spire of the Park Street Church. Among the rare books in this notable collection is the library of George Washington, purchased in 1848.

Several other important libraries were founded during the Victorian period as Boston became a great center of book collections. Of these, two should be mentioned: *The New England Historic Genealogical Society*, begun in 1845, and *The Boston Medical Library* in 1875. Both have become outstanding in their fields and are known throughout the world.

The Boston Public Library was the first large municipal library in the country to be open to the public. Founded in 1848, it was moved to Copley Square in 1895 to the new building designed by McKim, Mead, and White.

In the Victorian period Copley Square was framed by more architecturally important buildings than any other square in the country. Most of these buildings were of stone in the Gothic or Renaissance styles so that this part of Boston resembled a bit of old Florence.

Raised on a low stepped terrace, the handsome Renaissance-style library is built around a central courtyard. The symmetrical granite façade, splendid with a series of noble arched windows and entrance portals, overlooks the Square. Clusters of Strozzi-type lanterns with flaring spikes, inspired by those on the famous Florentine palace, flank the entrance. Carved panels by Saint-Gaudens with the seals of the library, the city, and the commonwealth as well as bronze doors executed by Daniel Chester French enrich the exterior. On the front terrace are two colossal bronze figures, representing Science and Art by Bela Pratt (1867–1917).

The center courtyard is framed on three sides of the ground floor by an arched loggia which provides a pleasant,

Courtyard of the Boston Public Library, 1895, by McKim,
Mead, and White

Bacchante *by Frederick MacMonnies (1865–1937)*

The Boston Public Library, 1895, Copley Square

shady place for reading in warm weather. A rectangular pool in the center was intended as a setting for a fountain. Charles Follen McKim ordered a bronze figure for the purpose to be presented to the library in memory of his wife, Julia Appleton McKim. This "Bacchante and Child" by the American sculptor Frederic MacMonnies (1863–1937) was executed in Paris and a copy was made for the Luxembourg Palace Gardens before the original was shipped to America. This graceful dancing nude figure created a furor in Boston. Some considered it immoral, indecent, and inappropriate for the adornment of the library so McKim withdrew his gift and gave it to the Metropolitan Museum in New York. In spite of the feeling of a few, others appreciated the statue, and George R. White ordered a copy which he gave to the Boston Museum of Fine Arts. This was set up in the garden court-

156

yard of the new building on Huntington Avenue where it may be seen today.

The interior of the great building covering an acre-and-a-half block is a repository of fine art as well as a storehouse for the famous collection of books. A grand staircase of yellow Siena marble, with wall paintings by P. Puvis de Chauvannes, leads to the lofty Bates Hall. This huge reading room, two hundred and eighteen feet in length, stretches across the entire front on the second floor. On the Huntington Avenue side a stately dark-paneled room forms the background for the well-known frieze paintings of the "Quest of the Holy Grail" by the British artist Edwin A. Abbey (1852–1911).

The third-floor stair hall, decorated with paintings of the "Triumph of Religion" by John Singer Sargent, leads to the Art and Architecture departments.

Branch libraries were opened in many sections of greater Boston. Library training courses were instituted at the main library in Copley Square and at Simmons College. More recent expansion brought the Children's Room, the music department's sound rooms, and other innovations to add to the already-established rooms.

Generous gifts of books and funds have expanded the collections through the years. One of the more recent benefactors was John Deferrari. Of Italian descent, he was born in humble circumstances in the North End. He used the Public Library extensively. In 1947, after amassing a fortune through investments, he left the Boston Public Library a million-dollar trust fund in appreciation. Many others have served the library well as trustees, directors, and in a variety of helpful ways. Due to their faith and devotion, the magnificent Boston Public Library remains a monument to learning and culture, a gem of architecture, and a great storehouse of art and books.

After the Civil War there was a steady decline in quality, design, and taste as rapid expansion and the speeding up of production resulted in a good deal of poor workmanship. There continued to be, however, outstanding examples of discrimination in architecture and other arts and crafts. The advancement in many fields in the Victorian era, especially in transportation, industry, science, horticulture, medicine, literature, music, and education, brought Boston to a position of distinction in the world.

Today the old culture and distinctive local characteristics are fast disappearing. The flavor of this unique city is being lost in the change to the standardized pattern of modern living. Larger, taller buildings — great cages of glass and metal — handsome and efficient, house us and our occupations.

Jet airplanes offer speedy transportation as they glisten in the sky and leave a long, floating ribbon of vapor over the city. Intricate new arteries and highways for express motor traffic are replacing the old roadways and buildings. Time-honored Boston moves on.

This is as it should be, if done with taste and distinction. The less significant of the older structures should give way to the new needs, but respect for the old is also important. Preservation does not mean just the saving of a building as such, but the saving for all time of those of architectural merit or of historical importance.

Historic sites and buildings remind us of great men and their wise decisions that made this wonderful free country. Let us not forget. Let us not destroy the significance of our heritage. Let us go forward with the integrity of our predecessors.

A SUGGESTED TOUR
OF VICTORIAN BOSTON

Begin at Boston Common and walk (following the endpaper map, numbers, and text) to *City Hall*. Proceed past *The Old Corner Book Store* and down State Street to *The Custom House*. (Open 9:00-11:30 A.M.; 1:30-4:00 P.M. every day except Saturday and Sunday). Take the elevator up the tower to the observation deck for a panoramic view of the water front.

Walk to the *places* nearby indicated on the map.

Drive along the Fitzgerald Expressway. Turn on Dover Street. See #8 on your left. Continue via Tremont Street to Broadway to Park Square and the *Emancipation* statue.

Proceed out Columbus Avenue one block to the *First Corps Cadet Armory*. Visit the collection of firearms.

Continue out Columbus Avenue; turn left on Clarendon Street to the dead end; jog left to Waltham Street and continue on to Washington Street. Turn right under the elevated-train structure to the *Cathedral of the Holy Cross*.

Turn right on Union Park Street to *Union Park*. Continue on to Tremont Street, turn left, and proceed to the traffic light, then left on West Dedham Street to Washington Street. Turn right on Washington Street and proceed to East Brookline Street; turn left.

Pause here at *Franklin Square* and continue on to Harrison Avenue. Turn right past #17 to *Worcester Square*.

Continue on to Columbus Avenue, and turn right on
Massachusetts Avenue to Huntington Avenue. Here, at
Symphony Hall, turn right past the *Horticultural Hall,
The First Church of Christ Scientist*, and the "French
Flats" to *Copley Square*. Note the vista down Hunting-
ton Avenue to *Trinity Church*.

Walk around the Copley Square area to the *Boston Public
Library*, the various churches, and other places of interest indicated on the map. Visit the Public Garden.

Walk in *The Back Bay* district to the churches and out Commonwealth Avenue to the *Hotel Vendome* and then over
to 137 Beacon Street to the *Gibson House*.

Drive out Commonwealth Avenue and turn left on Charles-
gate West to The Fenway. Turn left past *The Massachusetts Historical Society* and *Simmons College* to
Fenway Court, the *Gardner Museum*. Visit this important collection and enjoy the flowers and music on
Tuesdays, Thursdays, or Saturdays.

Conclude the tour at the *Museum of Fine Arts* nearby. Here,
in one of the most important museums in the world, are
many well-known and interesting collections.

See *The Book of Boston — Colonial Period* and *Federal Period* for
other tours and places of interest in Boston.

INDEX

162